"So many women struggle with their role as Christian wives, wondering how to achieve the marriage they've always dreamed of. With keen insight and compassion, Jen Weaver paints a realistic picture of biblical womanhood as it relates to marriage."

—**Jim Daly,** President, Focus on the Family

"*A Wife's Secret to Happiness* is the Christian marriage book for the millennial generation. Jen Weaver's heart for Jesus filters through each word as she authentically shares what living and loving biblically can do for your marriage. *A Wife's Secret to Happiness* tackles the biblical principles that are shunned by our culture and demonstrates the beauty of these principles for our marriages today. Throughout the book, Jen weaves the story of her own marriage and others' testimonies proving the wisdom of God's instructions for this ordained relationship. It's a must read for engaged and newly married women. A priceless gift."

—**Andy Lee,** author of *A Mary Like Me: Flawed Yet Called*

"Jen shares powerful insight into the opportunity for women to see their husbands through God's eyes and to champion them to live in their God-given identities and destinies. She reveals how aligning our dreams and marriages with God invites an overflow of his abundance, favor, and fulfillment, far beyond what we could conceive or achieve on our own. Jen celebrates the power and relief of surrendering our best to see God's best unfold in our marriages and lives, and empowers readers to do the same. A beautifully challenging read."

—**Robin Brady,** MA Psychology, Licensed Marriage and Family Therapist, Registered Art Therapist

"Jen Weaver has written an influential book for wives to know how to pursue and receive the blessings that God intends for them in marriage. She has a hilarious style of writing that's engaging, while offering insight through her personal hardships. She doesn't hesitate to share. Jen challenges wives to awaken their hearts to what God is doing in them and their marriage. I find her work to be relevant and encouraging, as both a wife and a counselor."

—**Ami Evans,** Licensed Professional Counselor, Owner of Ami Evans Counseling, Grapevine, Texas

"Freedom and hope are found in these pages! Reading *A Wife's Secret to Happiness* felt as though Jen had invited me to sit at her kitchen table and have coffee with her. Jen's welcoming candor, humor, and courage to address real issues head on is refreshing. Whether you are struggling to stay strong in a broken marriage or you are living in wedded bliss, this book is for you!"

—**Amy Ford,** President of Embrace Grace, Inc., author of *A Bump in Life*

"As a man I want to know who let 'The' Jen Weaver in on the secret thoughts and questions all men share about the mysteries related to our wives? Her insight into our world is very telling, and the way she casually demystifies it all in broad daylight is going to strongly help marriages. As a Pastor, I have to say I am very proud of Jen and the work, research, prayer, and reflection she has put into the book; it is filled with good writing, scriptural accuracy, healthy perspective, and positive encouragement."

—**Allan Kelsey,** Assoc. Sr. Pastor, Gateway Church

"Jen Weaver is absolutely wonderful. I love her heart for marriage and her message in *A Wife's Secret to Happiness*. The combination of biblical wisdom and practical resources make it a must read!"

—**Alli Worthington,** author of *Breaking Busy: Finding Peace and Purpose in A World of Crazy*

"This book is a beautiful symphony of the practical, spiritual, and applicable. Jen brilliantly weaves practical tips, including quizzes that test your 'wifestyle,' with honest examples, spiritual revelation, and realistic expectations. This book also contains amazing articles for application which only enhance the reading experience. As a therapist, many resources only contain pieces or parts that are useful; *A Wife's Secret to Happiness* is the full package. The reader is able to read any chapter in this book and gain valuable knowledge, insight, and practical application. I am excited to suggest it to my clients!"

—**Cassie Reid,** PhD, LPC-S, Lead Counselor, Cassie Reid Counseling

"This book made me laugh, cry, consider, and challenge myself to celebrate the gift of marriage in new ways. Jen's voice settles on you like a gracious friend across the kitchen table who loves you just because. Her wisdom, experience, and passion sink deep into the ink of every page, layering this book with the rich soil of God's loving and life-giving plan for marriage."

—**Kasey Van Norman,** bestselling author of *Named by God* and *Raw Faith*

To Lesley

A WIFE'S SECRET TO
happiness

Marie-José

2020

A WIFE'S SECRET TO

happiness

Receiving, Honoring, & Celebrating

God's Role for You in Your Marriage

JEN WEAVER

LEAFWOOD
PUBLISHERS
an imprint of Abilene Christian University Press

A WIFE'S SECRET TO HAPPINESS

Receiving, Honoring, & Celebrating God's Role for You in Your Marriage

LEAFWOOD
P U B L I S H E R S
an imprint of Abilene Christian University Press

Copyright © 2017 by Jen Weaver

ISBN 978-0-89112-433-7 | LCCN 2016041529

Printed in the United States of America

Published in association with The Blythe Daniel Agency, Inc., PO Box 64197, Colorado Springs, CO 80962.

LIBRARY OF CONGRESS CATALOGING-IN-PUBLICATION DATA
Names: Weaver, Jen, 1985- author.
Title: A wife's secret to happiness : receiving, honoring, and celebrating God's role for you in your marriage / Jen Weaver.
Description: Abilene : Leafwood Publishers, 2017.
Identifiers: LCCN 2016041529 | ISBN 9780891124337 (pbk.)
Subjects: LCSH: Wives—Religious life. | Marriage—Religious aspects—Christianity. | Sex role—Religious aspects—Christianity.
Classification: LCC BV4528.15 .W43 2017 | DDC 248.8/435—dc23
LC record available at https://lccn.loc.gov/ 2016041529

Cover design by ThinkPen Design, LLC | Interior text design by Sandy Armstrong

Leafwood Publishers is an imprint of Abilene Christian University Press
ACU Box 29138, Abilene, Texas 79699

1-877-816-4455 | www.leafwoodpublishers.com

20 21 22 / 7 6 5 4 3

Contents

Introduction

As a reader, I skip book introductions, so it won't hurt my feelings if you do the same. But if you want to hang out and chat a bit . . .

Welcome!

I'm Jen, and my husband, Jared, says I embody the cliché of living life like an open book. I'm doing my best to live up to that reputation in *A Wife's Secret to Happiness*, sharing lessons I've learned as a less-than-perfect wife in a less-than-perfect marriage blessed a hundred times over by the more-than-perfect provision of a loving Heavenly Father.

I've prayed, studied, and consumed concerning amounts of junk food as I typed my heart onto these pages. Punctuated with laughter and bittersweet tears, I aimed to pack truth and encouragement into every paragraph, uplifting your spirit and inspiring your marriage as we unfurl God's plan to empower our lives.

I'll be upfront, though: not all of these topics will taste sweet to your tongue. Some moments I'm sure to make you furious, especially as we confront societal norms with the truth of heaven's instruction. But to understand the secrets I've uncovered on my journey to happiness, please keep reading. Keep praying. **Ask the Lord what he wants you to receive, because there's a reason this book ended up in your hands.**

We welcome the Lord's provision through doing, not just reading, so please take notes. Make plans. Scribble all over these pages with reminders of what God stirs in your spirit as we explore **eleven specific blessings** he longs to gift to your life and marriage. We'll find **tips for practical application** as we compare conflicting **wifestyles**—the patterns that mark our tendencies as wives—and trade harmful habits for healthy ones. **Fun quizzes** and **discussion questions** personalize each theme and can aid your conversations with God, and perhaps with a book group, about how this content applies to you. Every chapter ends with a **powerful testimony from another real life wife** as she shares the freedom she's found by living according to the truth discussed in that section. In addition, anytime you see this icon ⊘ there's **exclusive bonus content** to download with worksheets and beautiful printable guides to use as you develop your wifestyle in accordance with God's Word.

Stepping from where we are today into the favor God supplies for tomorrow, next week, and next year requires intention and practical application. You carry powerful, purposeful dreams for your family's future. And the fulfillment you seek is precious and fathomless, not surface level.

I'm talking happiness more vibrant than the pleasant greetings and candle-blown wishes of a birthday. When we throw parties and eat cake, only to go back to regular life with work and chores, and pants that don't fit quite right because of yesterday's celebration.

Happiness more radiant than a wedding day. When blissful moments blur in the speed of the ceremony's passing. The commitment is real, but few wedding day moments resemble actual daily life.

No, for me and for you, I believe God offers joy that lasts. As we progress through the book, it's rare I even use the word *happy*. We can all relate to the desire for marital bliss, but I've found it's more accurate to label this yearning with stronger words. Unity. Provision. Safety. Intimacy. Partnership.

Contentment in these areas sneaks up on us. We're not standing outside any longer, nose pressed up against the glass, wishing we too could enjoy what others seem to have. No, we're busy getting involved in what Jesus calls us to—receiving, honoring, and celebrating his instruction so much that the sudden deep-rooted sense of satisfaction catches us by surprise. It's happened to me a thousand times, and God willing, it'll happen a million more. I live life as a wife through big, bold acts of faith and tiny little steps of obedience. And every once in a while, I look up and realize I've somehow walked myself into crazy favorable places, surrounded by the presence of Jesus.

CHAPTER ONE

The *Blessing* of Three Strands

"A cord of three strands is not quickly broken."

Ecclesiastes 4:12 NIV

Picture me wearing Manolos.

Yep, that's right. Bold. Modern. Romantic. I pair the gorgeous shoes with killer abs in couture gowns. My prince brings treasures from afar as little woodland creatures do my housework. Even my morning bedhead radiates beauty.

Do you ever wish married life worked like a fairy tale? Yep. Me too.

I chuckle as I write these words, cuddled on the love seat in my Texas-sized bedroom. Barefoot in shorts and a T-shirt, with two-day-old hair and an empty bag of mint chocolate Milanos. Hey, that's close to Manolos, right?

We know not to trust the fantasy of carriages and horsemen. Yet somewhere in our relationships, we've felt the draw to something more. Not something prettier—although we wouldn't mind—but something deeper. As a wife or bride-to-be, you've already heard the whisper in your spirit—the call to a marital experience different from what you've seen so far.

Maybe the rumble comes from places of disconnect. Knowing married life *could be* more—dare we believe, *should be* more—than the common parade. I'm talking about big things, finding commonalties past the shaky ground of shared interests. Life with a partner, not a roommate, and enjoying every aspect of intimacy—to intercourse and beyond.

We long to build marriages we love in the small moments. Not romanticized tales of perfect hair, homes, and husbands—because who can live up to that? I disqualify myself from my own daydream when he leaves dirty clothes on the floor or releases air biscuits in his sleep. We pretend not to notice these things, until pressure-cooked words erupt like Mount Vesuvius. Or maybe that's just me. We're looking for genuine joy in the middle of the mess and learning to make peace with each other's . . . quirks. Sound like something you want? Yep, me too. We need God's presence as the blessing of the third strand.

> We're looking for genuine joy in the middle of the mess.

Instead of moving toward it, we see God's plan for marriage fade into the distance. Our relationships are like boats out to sea without paddles, much less engines, adrift and taking on water. Every day I hear stories of betrayal, relationships heavy with anchors of broken promises. Once upon a time, they too wore love goggles. *Is it naïve to think my marriage will be any different?*

The question sticks in my throat, caught in the space between a wandering thought and legitimate concern.

I know we're created for something more. However, I still question it. Even my typing is timid. I place words on the page like fragile kisses when I want to engrave deep, permanent carvings. Our spousal relationships are crafted for divine callings, with purposes not relegated to powerless acts of contrition or the monotony of a somewhat satisfactory union. Not for painted on smiles and fake-it-till-you-make-it-or-die happiness, but life-giving communion with our husbands. We can experience joy even on days when we miss wedded bliss. The Lord wants that for us. Any promise in Scripture, all hope-filled encouragement found in Christ's love, is designed for his daughters, to move us from strength to strength.[1] Protected. Purposeful. Powerful.

In God's presence, we swap burdens for freedom.[2] We join the repetitive exchange of fears for faith, doubt for belief, and insecurity for confidence until we have nothing to trade any longer. A fullness we can't imagine.[3]

I hope you feel it—the freedom of God's plan as he etches it onto the tablet of your heart.

> Be strong and courageous. Do not be afraid or terrified . . .
> for *the LORD your God goes with you; he will never leave*
> *you nor forsake you.* (Deut. 31:6 NIV—emphasis mine)

My prayer is that the Lord shares his vision for your marriage through the pages of this book, just as he has with me.

If these words excite tingling nerves in your spirit, know I'm here with you, proclaiming, "Yep, me too!" God keeps talking with me about it—about the plan he has for marriage. An infusion of his power in a woman's connection with her husband, the way an electric current revives a lifeless heart.

I seek his voice because he promises to be found.[4] God will not call us anywhere his presence will not go with us. He won't ask us to do what he has not equipped us to complete. The Lord longs to lead our marriages into spacious places, interwoven with his peace and strength. God is the blessing of the third strand.

What Is a Third Strand?

You've no doubt heard of this illustrious fiber. A bond between two people may shatter with ease but "a cord of three strands is not quickly broken."[5] We often acknowledge the presence of the third strand through unity candles or comingling elements on a wedding day, but we miss the grandness of this coupling if we relegate it to a symbolic act. Marriage is more than a ceremony. Gloriously more.

God wasn't a guest at your wedding. The day you made your vows, he participated in active agreement, invisible yet majestic in glory. If a pastor officiated your ceremony, he or she said something like, "Dearly beloved, we are gathered here today *in the sight of God* and these witnesses to join this man and this woman in holy matrimony." You stood with your man just as I did with mine. By our actions we said, "God, he is the one." And the Lord joined us to our husbands.[6]

The Almighty wasn't distracted by my grandiose daydreams of life as a wife. He knew all the hard times to come, the difficult conversations and painful circumstances. The Lord saw the days when I wouldn't want to consider Jared better than myself,[7] or forgive as I have been forgiven.[8] Yet he stood as witness to our union, providing a resounding "so be it" in the heavens as we vowed to honor and cherish for as long as we both shall live.

> The threads of his tapestry hold our marriage together when everything else unravels.

My vows weren't foolish promises, although in challenging moments I question my sanity. God's third strand compensates for where we lack. The divine design of marriage necessitates his daily involvement because we can't uphold our solemn words without him. The threads of his tapestry hold our marriage together when everything else unravels.

To prepare for our pending nuptials, Jared and I wrote our own wedding vows. I spent hours guzzling lattes, making every attempt to draft passionate yet feasible affirmations. Noble, heart-moving words felt most appropriate, but I had a better chance at becoming Wonder Woman than fulfilling lofty proclamations.

"I will always honor and respect you." *Always? Maybe sometimes.*

"I will submit to you joyfully as the head of our family." *Umm . . . I'll try not to fight against your leadership? Yeah, that sounds encouraging.*

Expecting to fail was to admit defeat before we even began. But to preface each vow with "I will try" was a worse alternative. With flushed cheeks and a diverted gaze, I admitted this concern during premarital counseling, hoping for supernatural insight, or at least a superhero cape.

"Vows are hard," our pastor said.

A wedding happens once. Each day afterward is an opportunity to say, "I *still* do." Choosing permanence in our marriages and proclaiming "Amen and Amen" to ourselves when it comes time to practice the promises we made. Vows represent what we work toward and strive for throughout our entire marriage. Some promises are all or nothing—you either protect fidelity or you don't. But others endure as works in progress as we learn to love and honor each other. No wonder we need God's company.

When two work together, we get a better return.[9] We share strength and warmth. But what happens when the bed is cold?

When one falls because the other pushed them, or isn't around to help them stand again? When a bride works on her marriage solo, her nerves and energy soon fray. As I walked down the aisle on my wedding day, I didn't picture "becoming one" with my husband through terse conversations and irrational reactions. That's the value of the third strand—when one or both of you fail, God picks you up. Even better than the *important* faith-filled loyalty one spouse shows another is the Lord's faithfulness to your union. You are not alone. He longs to hold the fragile moments of your relationship, to fortify delicate bonds with the tight-knit fabric of his presence.

The Invitation

God wants to be involved in our marriages—praise his holy name!—but we must *include* him. In the same way he grants free will to receive salvation, he will not force his involvement in our homes. As a Gentleman, the Lord waits for me to invite him into my relationship. And I'm good at shutting the door in his face.

Remember that glimpse into my life from earlier? Me curled on the sofa in desperate need of cookies and, someday, a nice long shower? I'm still here, but this time I'm pouting. Not that immature jutted-chin-and-diva-hair-toss petulance. The justified kind—if there was such a thing. I mumble complaints about "Jared doesn't notice" and "Is he listening?" and defend my quiet protest as "prayer." Who else would I be talking to, sitting in a room by myself?

Then I hear Jesus. His voice echoes down a long corridor because sometimes I need the *dramatic* so I'll pay attention.

"I'm waiting in the hallway. Are you done, so you can let me in?"

Now, I know God is everywhere. He knows all things, discerns all thoughts, and hears every word.[10] But I also know that thinking and talking are different than praying. Scripture tells me that God gives good gifts to his kids.[11] Better than blue Tiffany boxes or fancy cars. *Good* gifts. The kind only he can give. Peace beyond understanding,[12] hope without measure,[13] and supernatural provision. Blessing a marriage with sincere harmony and happiness.

He says I don't have because I don't ask. Or my requests are selfish, looking to spend his generosity on my own pleasures.[14] He's right. I default to depending on my strength, advocating for my preferences, and I work hard to achieve my own results. It takes such arduous efforts to "fix" my marriage, to set us up for *my* version of success:

- Tearing down molehills to prevent future mountains
- Exhaustively talking through problems with few results
- Feeling like I'm the only one trying—and if I let go it will all fall apart

I catch some soft murmurs of "Yep, me too." While I'm sorry for your pain, it's good to know we're not alone. No one signs up for this hardship.

We crave rare and exquisite marriages, spilling over with knowing and loving and being together. Not standing in proximity, but cherished in unity. Instead, bone-weary women experience great loss. We're at a loss for words. For strength. For direction and resources. Whatever we achieve is held with beautiful vise-gripped hands, fingernails digging scars into our palms for fear that we'll lose what we fought so hard to gain.

We must let God be the third strand.

> The Lord's presence changes my marriage, and I am a gatekeeper.

The Lord's presence changes my marriage, and I am a gatekeeper. I hold keys to offer him access not just to the *ceremony* on the first day but to the *relationship* for each day that comes after.

No fiber of God's Holy Being is passive. To include his strand in my relationship cord means I receive him as my Leader. He goes before to prepare the way. God isn't that lame camp counselor that shouts instructions from the shaded picnic bench as you sweat out the obstacle course on your own. The King of Heaven, Creator of the universe, invests his power and authority in our marital success. He blesses our union in ways that far surpass human ability or achievement.

Receiving the Blessing

But here's the deal. In the same breath as "Please, God," we say, "No, thank you."

"Oh, *that's* your plan to bless my marriage? Never mind."

We make the same mistake as this guy Naaman[15] in Scripture, although here I take some creative liberties with his story.

In the days of 2 Kings chapter 5, #Naaman is always trending. A Syrian army commander in high favor with the king, God grants him success in his military career. He has a wife, servants, and a prestigious job, so I imagine his life is pretty lavish for his day. Plus, his subtitle is "mighty man of valor," so you know he has things going for him.

But Naaman also has an itchy and rather painful affliction, plagued by an embarrassing skin disease that no lotion, potion, treatment, or doctor can rid him of. He tries to conceal the discomfort, but everyone can tell. We're not talking dandruff or the occasional sunburn; Naaman's skin oozes grossness.

As days turn to weeks, then months, Naaman continues through the stages of grief as he accepts this health issue as a way of life. Then he hears of a supernatural cure. The God of Israel can heal him through his prophet Elisha. Well, Mr. Man of Valor knows some people who know some people, and gets himself invited to meet the prophet to be healed. Naaman marvels at his good fortune on the journey from Syria to Israel, grateful that his friend, the king, can apparently call in favors with the God of the Israelites.

His processional makes the final turn in front of Elisha's house, with rows of regal chariots pulled by his most elegant horses.

Picking at a scab on his arm, Naaman mutters to himself, "I overdid the entourage, but I want to show this guy that I'm worth his time."

He folds himself out of the chariot and stretches. The stress of a long journey shows on his face, but his weary eyes gleam with excitement. This is his moment. His miracle.

The best way to describe Naaman's attire is *luxurious*. Picture Prada for the biblical era. Naaman looks good, and he knows it. He straightens his garments and struts up to the house with the same victory swagger as when he's victorious in battle, tired but eager for whatever fantastical display of power awaits.

The doors fling open and out steps a servant, sent by Elisha. Naaman's expression tightens, but he holds his tongue. He is the commander of the Syrian army, and this prophet dares to send a mere servant!

One sentence is all he's given: "Go wash in our river."

Naaman storms away from the home, fists clenched and shouting things I won't repeat. Dirty river water is not the wondrous sign he expected. He could have bathed in a bunch of rivers back in Syria. He came all this way, to this God, for something dazzling, not something dull. Definitely not something degrading.

Thankfully, Naaman's servants encourage him. "What if the prophet had told you to do something great? Wouldn't you have done it? Climbed a mountain. Fought an enemy. Traveled the world for the right ingredients to craft a new lotion. Fasted and prayed and wept and worshiped. Those things might not have worked anyway. Why not do this thing?"

When Naaman finishes his swim in the Jordan River, he's healed, and God creates the first antiaging treatment known to man.

Good times, right? Such an extraordinary outcome for an ordinary action. Similar to Naaman, we too can become unreceptive to God's offering of healing and blessings in our lives. While we want God's presence and leadership in our marriages, with the high rate of divorce and the even higher number of troubled relationships, the odds of a happy marriage are stacked against us. We long for confidence in our spousal connection, free from doubt or fear. We pray for godly husbands to offer safety and security in our homes. For God to fulfill our dreams and callings. To live in complete unity with our mate, enjoying the haven of the most intimate human relationship God created. We ask to have his blessing run to and through our marriages, and his affirmative answer is as undesirable and undeniable as a call to jump in the Jordan River.

Here comes the choice: to let in the blessing of the third strand, or to put him back in the hallway.

You may choose to leave the Lord in the entryway from time to time as he reveals his design for marriage with your husband as the leader in your home. God wants your relationship to start and stay on solid ground, but when we talk about the dirty "S" word of submission, you may consider leaving me out in the hallway, too. Public opinion distorts many truths in God's Word. Submission is divine empowerment that culture has confused and the enemy has contorted to mean oppression. Its blessing is misunderstood and refused by those who've never seen God cleanse the skin of a leper in the murky waters of a riverbank. But what happens when we choose the blessing of the third strand by submitting to God and also to our husbands? Are you willing to follow God on this new adventure? To receive his blessings for your marriage? Yep, me too.

Building Wifestyle Habits

Every choice contributes to our "wifestyle"–the pattern we establish for ourselves as married women. If we don't live with intention, our wifestyle can become . . . unbecoming . . . as we develop unhealthy perspectives, attitudes, and habits in interactions with our husbands. Obedience to God's instruction aligns us with his will, allowing us to receive the blessings he desires to impart in our lives. Disobedience earns the opposite result.

In the pages ahead, we'll look at redefining our wifestyles by establishing healthy habits to align ourselves with God's blessings for our marriages. Jesus has plans for your husband, and an anointing to place on your life as a wife.

Wifestyle: Frayed or Braided

The frayed wife is often worn-out. She finds it difficult to include God in the day-to-day circumstances of her marriage and wishes he'd just show up rather than wait to be invited. Her husband may resist her efforts to improve their connection, leaving her feeling lonely and underappreciated. She's determined to have a happy marriage and sees every issue as an obstacle to struggle through and overcome. The frayed wife is strong and resolute but finds minimal results.

The braided wife chooses a marriage interwoven with the presence of Jesus, even when God's instruction, circumstances, or even her husband prove difficult. She views Christ as an integral and practical part of interactions with her spouse. While her marriage requires hard work, she sees it as a joy and as a partnership with both God and her husband. Peace and prayer mark her approach and interactions. Her spousal connection carries God's grace—making it easier to work through the hardest circumstances.

Is Your Wifestyle Frayed or Braided?

Complete this wifestyle quiz to personalize the themes of this chapter in a practical way. Please circle the responses below that best represent your answer to each question.

Our development as believers and as wives is a lifelong process, and you may find yourself at different points in the wifestyle spectrum. This isn't a grading scale—I'm talking to you, fellow Type A personalities. We are all a mix of both wifestyle habits. Don't read them like labels or boxed-in categories. The goal is to provide tangible markers to help us identify and improve current habits and perspectives.

BONUS: Would you rather not write in your book? Download printable versions of the wifestyle quizzes at thejenweaver.com/wifestylebonus

	A	B
I find it tiring to work on my marriage.	True	False
When I consider the past week, I've spent more time *talking* about issues in my marriage than *praying* about them.	True	False
I struggle to make intentional choices to rely on Jesus when interacting with my husband.	True	False

	A	**B**
I frequently suggest ways my husband can improve his bad habits.	True	False
Please circle words in each column that best describe your recent attitudes or behaviors. Circle all that apply.	Complaining Pouting Frustrated	Grateful Prayerful Renewed

Please tally your results. If you have more "A" answers, you exhibit a frayed wifestyle. "B" answers show a braided wifestyle.

If you sense even a hint of condemnation during this exercise, that's not from God. Squish those lies with the truth of Jesus. Roll the book up and use it like a fly swatter if you have to.

> There is therefore now no condemnation for those who are in Christ Jesus. (Rom. 8:1)

Condemnation brings guilt and shame. Conviction brings repentance—the opportunity to think again and choose a different course. That's what we're doing: thinking again and choosing differently. Wash. Rinse. Repeat.

Ways to Grow as a Braided Wife

A braided wife can use the following steps to live with God's third strand as an integral part of her marriage:

- Spend time in prayer. When you're tempted to grumble to yourself or complain to another person about issues in your marriage, choose to pray about them instead. Consider carrying an index card to write your prayer list for later.
- When your husband annoys you most, ask God to bless him. I don't mean, "Lord, let him get what's coming." Pray

for every blessing you can think of: his health, job, ministry, and spiritual walk. Pray for the acne on his face or weird patch of hair on his back. Let grace and gratitude replace any negative emotion.

- Create reminders for yourself to keep the door open for God's presence in your marriage. Use sticky notes to put verses with God's promises in strategic places for you to see throughout the day. Schedule time to talk with God about upcoming decisions, or set alarms on your phone to check your wifestyle habits and God's leadership in various moments. Are you #wifestylin right now?
- Write out the top five pain points in your marriage. Ask God to talk with you about why they hurt you and what he wants to do about them. Gain insight from the Lord about how he sees these problems; *then* petition for God's help according to his plan.
- Make intentional choices to build trust in God's leadership. Read Bible verses outlining his promises. List ways he's been there for you. You may want to read the Scripture references noted in the endnotes for this chapter. Ask God to continue talking with you about the blessing of three strands in your marriage.

What Do You Think?

- Is married life what you thought it would be like when you were dating or engaged? How is it the same? In what ways is it different?
- Between frayed and braided, which wifestyle is dominant in your life right now? How is this evidenced in your daily life?

- Is God convicting you about anything that you'd like to repent of? What is the different choice you will make moving forward?
- What excites you most about the blessing of three strands?

Real Life #Wifestylin: Lori's Story

John and I officially began our relationship in August 2007. He proposed in December 2008 and the wedding was set for July of 2009—our life was to grow together from that day forward. Marriage, home, and babies . . . I had it planned. Problem is, life doesn't always go as we plan. A month before he proposed, John got a fabulous new job in Houston, Texas. He felt taking this job was the right decision, even though I was still in nursing school, stuck in Baton Rouge, Louisiana. So I chose to trust God and follow my soon-to-be husband into the unknown.

We married in July (as planned), but there was no moving in with my life-mate. I stayed in Baton Rouge for the first six months of our marriage, trusting God and walking by faith that he would strengthen a marriage established apart and would reward us for following him. In December 2009 I graduated nursing school, and after months of tears and trusting God, we were finally together . . . sort of. John's job required him to travel Monday through Friday every week. I thought the tears had ended when I moved in, but they only increased. Here I was in a new city, in a new church, with no friends, and all alone. I was so frustrated, yet in prayer we knew we were walking the right path.

God proved faithful! We bought a house and had two beautiful children. God became ever more real and close as my dependence shifted from my husband to my Heavenly Father! I learned to find my strength in God. In giving God my marriage and submitting to my husband's leadership for our family, I became a stronger individual. Here I stand, closer to God, stronger in spirit, happy, and filled with life. The road has been long and hard, but I wouldn't change it. I could have quit, or made John quit to please me, to stay where I was "comfortable." Instead, I chose to follow my husband and place my life, marriage, and family in God's hands. Standing on the other side, I am a woman blessed beyond measure!

–Lori, married in 2009

Perhaps you can relate to Lori's struggles when circumstances didn't match her idealized life plan. God's ways are *always* better than ours, but we must choose to put our dependence on him to receive the blessings he has in store. My prayer is that you will also connect with Lori's victories as the Lord functions as the third strand in your marriage.

CHAPTER TWO

The *Blessing* of a Godly Husband

"Husbands, love your wives, as Christ loved
the church and gave himself up for her . . ."

Ephesians 5:25

The valiant knight approaches. His polished armor glimmers in the moonlight, outshining the beauty of his ivory steed as he races to free the damsel from her distress.

The princess swoons, "Oh my hero. My savior."

And I gag. Please join me in an eye roll of disgust. Jesus as Savior is a given, but I don't need the rescue or domineering rule of a Prince Charming.

I want the love of a godly man . . . in theory. In practicality, I've spent most of my marriage fighting against such a blessing.

For the husband is the head of the wife as Christ is the head of the church, his body, of which he is the Savior. (Eph. 5:23 NIV)

Champion or Conqueror?

God created safety in numbers. Adam is better with Eve.[1] The Lord shows up when two or more are gathered in his name,[2] and a pair of workers earns a greater return.[3]

Many wives struggle with the visual of headship in marriage. If my husband is the head, what does that make me? The exhausted, aching, standing-barefoot-in-the-kitchen-with-the-children feet? Nope.

We'll talk about unity under Christ in the next chapter, but for now, let's use an analogy offered by Biblical commentator, Matthew Henry, to describe spousal connection: "Eve was not taken out of Adam's head to top him, neither out of his feet to be trampled on by him, but out of his side to be equal with him, under his arm to be protected by him, and near to his heart to be loved by him."[4] The blessing of a godly husband offers sacrificial leadership, love, and safety.

A woman longs for security just as, deep down, a man desires to offer it. Husband-leadership has nothing to do with dominance or superiority. The man who seeks to conquer his wife isn't a hero. Unintentional or not, he's a villain. Recognizing your husband as the head of your family does not give license for abuse, mistreatment, or lesser esteem of you as a wife. Our husbands have the privilege of offering protection and empowerment. Their calling as leaders allows them to care for us—a role of service, not male chauvinism.

The role of a husband is to champion his wife's cause, not conquer her. As the leader of our home, my husband is one who fights on my behalf. He is my defense, adding safety so I may live with a double measure of boldness. He makes me brave when I face the enemy. And through his partnership I receive the courage to dream bigger.

If your husband is abusive or forces you into sin, he has abdicated his role as your leader and misused his position for selfish gain. Abuse is not a passing cold that will get better with time. It's a cancer to you and to your marriage—sucking out every bit of health and leaving only destruction in its wake. Maltreatment isn't limited to physical injury. It includes untreated substance abuse and mental health issues; unrepentant infidelity; and fiscal, emotional, spiritual, mental, sexual, and verbal cruelty. The promised blessings and benefits of healthy wifestyle habits remain true, but your solo actions cannot heal the wounds in your relationship.

God *can* redeem your marriage, and you need external guidance to help bring you and your spouse to a place of health. If this section applies to your life, know that I'm praying for you. Please seek help from a Christian counselor or organization that ministers specifically to this need.

When I go up against life's obstacles, daunting circumstances shout back at me, *Oh yeah? You and what army?* It's me and this guy, I motion. As partners for life, we fight as a team. Through our unity we come under the banner of the King of Kings, so it's heaven's warriors you'll contend with. You little bullies don't stand a chance, even in the craziest of circumstances.

The Stranger in My Shower

Like many young couples, Jared and I enjoyed our newlywed season on a tight budget. Our limited allowances shrank even smaller with the decision to fulfill a lifelong dream—to backpack through Europe. After three years of penny-pinching and generic brand shopping, we left our little apartment for a month-long adventure.

Our extravagant journey proved far from luxurious as we roomed in hostels—not hotels—with accommodations reminiscent of high school summer camp. One day, while taking an afternoon shower in a Venice hostel, I found myself alone in a spacious girl's locker-room-style bathroom. At last, a quiet moment to myself. The water had almost turned warm when a tall, broad profile appeared on the shower curtain.

"Hello, woman." His deep accent rattled my knees as his shadow reached for the hanging divide.

I posed to fight and shouted at the top of my lungs. Thankfully, my voice came out more battle cry than mousy squeak, causing him to flee from the room. Within seconds, I stood with Jared, my wet skin crawling inside sticky clothes.

The anger on Jared's face that afternoon has remained unmatched in the tenure of our relationship. As if he transformed into a fierce creature under the light of a full moon. You know that passage about how if one man falls he has the other to help him up?[5] Well, if one woman gets peeped on in the shower, she has her husband to lay the smackdown.

> If one woman gets peeped on in the shower,
> she has her husband to lay the smackdown.

We scoured the hostel with hostile diligence, me following behind as my beloved hunted through each dorm. With a cold trail and zero evidence, we chalked the event up to a youth prank and reported it to hostel authorities. Recalling my kung fu shower pose, it felt *good* to have handled things on my own. It felt *better* not to have to.

Sometimes we associate a husband-champion with wife-weakness and assume that when it comes time to fight, we need to drop and huddle in the corner, hoping our men will save us before it's too late. Other times, we withhold opportunities for our husbands to partner with us. Afraid of what it means to need or want their support, we allow the enemy to regroup and try again as we return to our isolated showers.

The blessing of a godly husband means receiving our men as demonstrations of God's favor in our lives. The marital roles of husband and wife are established as the Lord's provision, and he has called your mate to lead, love, and serve you. While this chapter is about the benefits of a godly husband, it's not written for our men to read. *This content is for us.* So in the midst of our conversations with God, in the direction he brings and new wifestyle changes we make, we can reference a holy measuring stick.

> Husbands, love your wives, just as Christ loved the church and gave himself up for her to make her holy, cleansing her by the washing with water through the word, and to present her to himself as a radiant church, without stain or wrinkle or any other blemish, but holy and blameless. (Eph. 5:25–27 NIV)

Live according to *that* promise. Your man gets to be *that guy* for you. The standard of a good husband, a godly husband, has nothing to do with the marriage we picture in romantic daydreams. It's not measured by the successes of another relationship, or tested against the ooey gooeyness of the Hallmark channel. Your husband *is* the Ephesians 5 guy. Don't be discouraged if he's not there yet, if he's unaware of what you need right now, or if you're better at sparring with each other than taking down the enemy together. God always equips us to complete our calling, and your husband is set apart to love you.

> God always equips us to complete our calling,
> and your husband is set apart to love you.

Love

Scripture says, "Husbands, love your wives,"[6] and all the married women shout, "Amen!"

But in Jen's dictionary, marital love is defined in all sorts of crazy ways. Love is never cleaning the bathroom because you've done it for me. Eating off your plate because I don't order as well as you. The blissful illusion of extra sleep because you get up first. Love is you reading my mind to know when I mean what I say and when I'm saying things because I'm mad. It's asking me what's wrong, even when it means we'll argue. Love is flowers and heart-shaped boxes of chocolate and rom-com movies and back rubs that are just back rubs not lead-ins to something else. Because you know I'm tired and sexpectations give me headaches.

While I'm wandering down this buffet line of definitions, I'd prefer such affection came from a "godly" man whose choices align with my preferences. By the time I reach the dessert bar, I haven't described love or God at all. I've only detailed my selfish desires—the opposite of love, the antithesis of God.

> Husbands, love your wives, as Christ loved the church
> and gave himself up for her. (Eph. 5:25)

Praise Jesus, Hallelujah. A godly husband loves like Jesus loved when he *died* for his bride. Cue the movie montage of great romantic gestures: Jack sinking with the *Titanic* because he left the entire floating board for Rose, even though they could have shared it. Noah reading the story of their romance to Allie in hopes that *The Notebook* would bring back a moment's recognition of their love. And we can't forget Westley's willingness to sacrifice everything for his *Princess Bride*. Such unhindered abandon appeals to me. I don't want Jared to actually lose his life for mine, but I wouldn't mind if he cherished me as worthy of the cost. In many ways, a husband has the harder job. Sure Ephesians 5 calls wives to respect our spouses—we'll talk more about that later—but men are called to give themselves completely.

> In the same way husbands should love their wives as their own bodies. He who loves his wife loves himself. For no one ever hated his own flesh, but nourishes and cherishes it, just as Christ does the church . . . (Eph. 5:28–29)

A man shows that he values himself through steadfast devotion to his wife. As women, we may chuckle at this notion. *Yeah, if he knows what's good for him.*

Guess what? God agrees. If a man pays attention, he'll recognize that to trample on his wife is to stomp on his own head. Two are now one.[7] To cherish her is to value himself and to demean her is to degrade himself. In the hardcore, awe-inspiring way Christ—who died for the world—loves, husbands should cherish their wives. Not just in affinity or affection. Established deeper than fondness or momentary passion from an infatuated heart, this love calls men to esteem, value, and devote themselves to their wives just as Christ esteemed, valued, and devoted himself to the church.

The true blessing of a godly husband has little to do with a honey-do list or romantic gestures. It's good for your husband to show affectionate consideration. For him to honor you through the way he spends his time, appreciates your beauty, lives as your best friend, and helps around the house. But focusing on these actions makes us like little kids on Christmas morning—distracted by big boxes and shiny wrapping paper while ignoring the gifts inside.

Best Friends Forever

The world would have us think that when we picked our husbands we simply married our best friends. That your marriage certificate only names the man you want to *romance* you for the rest of your life. The one authorized to see you naked, father your children, and partner with you on life adventures.

That's just the shiny box.

As Christ is a gift to the church, a husband is a gift to his wife—not a pretty package to sit on the shelf, but a transformative offering. A sacrificial present who gives of himself to present us back to Jesus as holy and blameless. A godly husband doesn't stop at making me *feel* beautiful. He *makes* me beautiful, cleansing me by washing me with water through the Word.[8] He presents me to Jesus as a radiant bride, without blemish. Holy and blameless.[9]

That's the part I've been fighting, because I prefer leadership I can keep at arm's length. We all have leaders: work supervisors, church pastors, ministry overseers, government officials, mentors, coaches, Bible study teachers, and accountability partners. Their oversight is compartmentalized to specific hours or activities. We decide if we want their guidance, changing departments, teams, or churches when necessary. We choose how often we see them, when we listen, and what we disclose.

> If I wanted a godly husband, I'd stop disqualifying him from the leadership role in my life and encourage him to walk in it.

Husbands are permanent. We live behind the veil, exposed and vulnerable. I default to wanting a friendly husband, not a godly one. A peer to carry my secrets, not offer correction. If I wanted a godly husband, I'd stop disqualifying him from the leadership role in my life and encourage him to walk in it.

Scripture says to confess our sins to one another that we may be healed.[10] So why do I first think to confess to another believer, and not to my spouse? Do I doubt that he, too, as a member of the body of Christ, offers forgiveness? Will I let him hold me blameless?[11]

Do I see my husband as trusted counsel? One who can partner with the Holy Spirit to bring proper application of God's Word in my life? Or do I turn to other people for advice and consensus first, coming to my husband to share my completed plan, without asking him to seek God with me?

Deep down, I want my guy to be *that guy*. The one who knows my weaknesses and loves me anyway. Who sees my failings and offers gentle instruction. Who senses insecurities and brings encouragement. But in the day-to-day, I hide. I mask pain, justify mistakes, and combat his words with harsh critique. I want a friendly man, not a godly one.

When I limit my husband to flowery, shiny, romantic love, I miss out on the gift he is in my life. I reject the blessing of a godly husband because I'm so busy sprinting here and there, seeking external guidance and input, that I've forgotten that marriage means throwing away your running shoes.

BONUS: Download this helpful article "When You Question Your Husband's Counsel" at thejenweaver.com/wifestylebonus

Leave and Cleave: Toss Your Running Shoes

Some of you will put down this book, clutching your hard-earned triathlon medals for dear life. Come back! I'm talking about symbolic sneakers, not real ones. The kind you lace up to run to your parent's house in the middle of a spousal argument. Cross-trainers reminiscent of your single days, where you could go where and do what you wanted. Every new adventure carried the romantic prospect of *what could be* instead of the sometimes mundane of *what is.*

"Therefore a man shall leave his father and mother and
hold fast to his wife, and the two shall become one flesh."
(Eph. 5:31)

It's hard to hold fast to someone when you're running away. That's why the verse starts with *leaving.* Both husband and wife must transition from one lifestyle to another—from single to married, and for some of us, from childhood into adulthood.

*Step #1: **Honor.*** Holding fast to your husband doesn't mean dishonoring your folks. Married life means adjusting our connections, not cutting off all communication with our families. Speak well of them. Be intentional in how you continue your family relationships and forgive past grievances so your husband won't inherit those wounds.

The concept of honor also comes into play if we default to preferring Mom or Dad over our spouse, thus dishonoring our men by diminishing the value of their voice, perspective, or presence in our lives.

*Step #2: **Overcoming conflict.*** Don't tattle on your husband, especially to your family. The negative things you share in the heat of an emotional moment may cause permanent damage to their relationship with your husband. Your parents will always want what is best for you, and it's possible their feedback will also hinder conflict resolution. Imagine if your mom's voice echoed in your head every time you argued with your mate: *You deserve better. . . . He's the one at fault. . . . I hate to see you so unhappy.* Seek unbiased counsel when needed. One-sided allies won't do any good for you or your marriage.

*Step #3: **Priorities.*** Leaving your parents and fastening yourself to your husband means he is your new priority. Your loyalty belongs to one another. Discuss the new traditions you want in your life together. This includes holidays, church membership, and any other traditions once enjoyed by your individual families. Leaving and cleaving doesn't mean you need to move to another state or that you can't go to Grandpa's house for Christmas. Establish a new home as husband and wife with your new family unit as the priority. Children are instructed to obey their parents.[12] Now married, we are still called to honor but not to obey. It's not dishonorable to hear Dad's recommendations and choose otherwise. Receive wisdom and make choices in line with God's direction and priorities. Your parents may not understand your decisions, and that's OK; the path you forge as a new family unit takes precedence.

Step #4: Economics. You haven't left home if your parents bankroll your lifestyle. Living like adults means living within our means, and we can't get upset if our parents still treat us like children while they're doing our laundry and paying our cell phone bills. Allowing your folks to subsidize your income may seem convenient, but this dependence throws your relationships off-balance.

You'll notice that the steps above form the acronym HOPE. Leaving the world of our childhoods and cleaving to our spouses is a strenuous process. The difficulty multiplies when it seems like we're leaving but our men are still clinging to momma's apron strings. When that happens, choose HOPE.

BONUS: Download the HOPE Worksheet at
thejenweaver.com/wifestylebonus

We also must cut ties with the familiarity of our single lives and learn to honor one another in the small ways. Jared and I struggled with this early in our marriage, since we both spent several years living as single adults. Building spousal consideration into our daily habits takes intentional effort, in things like coordinating schedules or considering each other's preferences.

> The blessed annoyance of married life is that everything is a process.

The blessed annoyance of married life is that everything is a process. Building unity. Becoming one. Transforming into the likeness of Christ. Developing healthy habits and wifestyles. Our job is to believe God, receiving his promises for our lives and marriages, and to have hope, even when the fruition of these callings seems a long way off. Our perspectives impact more than we may think.

BONUS: Read the article "Creating Family Traditions and Building New Memories" at thejenweaver.com/wifestylebonus

The Home Disadvantage

During his ministry, Jesus traveled from town to town performing miracles. He healed the sick, raised the dead, and cast out demons, real Son-of-God-like stuff. But he was unable to perform miracles when he returned to his hometown of Nazareth. So much for a home-field advantage.

I'm not a big sports fan, but I know the basics. Football has yards and goals. Baseball makes you run bases during innings. And teams love the supportive fans and familiar facilities of *home advantage*. Unfortunately, Jesus found hometown ministry disadvantageous because his townsfolk's familiarity with him hindered their belief.

In Mark chapter 1, Jesus travels to Capernaum where he frees a man from an unclean spirit and then visits Simon's house and restores health to Simon's mother-in-law who "lay ill with a fever" (Mark 1:29–31). Jesus moves on to other towns "preaching in their synagogues and casting out demons" (Mark 1:39). In one such town, he cures a leper and news of the healing traveled, "so that Jesus could no longer openly enter a town, but was out in desolate places, and people were coming to him from every quarter" (Mark 1:45).

Jesus returns to Capernaum and heals a paralytic in Mark chapter 2. In Mark 3, he heals a man's withered hand, and then in Mark 4, Jesus teaches at the sea and calms the storm with a command. In Mark 5, he comes into the country of the Gerasenes to heal a man with a demon, and then crosses back to the other side to heal a woman with an issue of blood and raise Jairus's daughter from the dead.

After all these exploits, the crowds, and numerous miracles of a successful evangelistic tour, we arrive at Mark chapter 6. I picture a homecoming parade as Christ enters Nazareth. Shops close early. A bandstand is set up in the square, where the mayor prepares to present Jesus with a key to the town stables. Fans carry balloons and wear "I grew up with Jesus" T-shirts.

Things happened a little differently.

> "Is not this the carpenter, the son of Mary and brother of
> James and Joses and Judas and Simon? And are not his
> sisters here with us?" And they took offense at him. . . .
> And he could do no mighty work there, except that he
> laid his hands on a few sick people and healed them. And
> he marveled because of their unbelief. (Mark 6:3, 5–6)

I imagine the outrage growing as townsfolk share stories of the early years. The babysitter offers candid photographs. The town physician recalls Christ's annual physicals and how he detested multivitamins. An old man brings out a rickety chair—Jesus's first project in Joseph's shop. *Who does he think he is, to teach and perform miracles?*

Christ carried power into his hometown. Authorized by God to perform works mightier than healing the sick, which in my mind is still a big deal. Imagine what could have happened in Nazareth if they believed in God's call on Christ's life.

Mark chapter 6, verse 5, Jesus could do no mighty work.

Verse 6, he leaves.

Verse 7, he calls the twelve disciples and sends them out with authority to cast out demons and heal the sick. Jesus didn't lose power when he stepped foot in his old stomping grounds. The people simply rejected his ministry. Their familiarity with Christ's past kept him from ministering to them according to his present calling.

As a wife, you are part of your husband's ministry. God calls him to lead and love you. Your man is charged with authority to do you good, and some of us are stuck like doubting townspeople.

Isn't this the same guy who [insert annoying habit or area of temptation]?

Where would he even learn to lead the way I need him to?

He's a supervisor at work or church, but hasn't proven to be a leader at home.

If other people knew what I know, they wouldn't receive his oversight either.

Don't be distracted by your mate's backstory. We reject the blessings of a godly husband when we disqualify our men from receiving God's call to lead. The Lord placed him in your life for your good.

Wifestyle: Short or Venti

A wife determines how much she will receive from her husband. She can choose a "venti" portion of God's favor through his leadership, or only accept a "short" cup—a marriage in title but not blessed in the abundance of God's anointing.

A short wifestyle is marked by discouragement and disbelief toward husband-leadership. She defines love and happiness in her relationship by her own preferences, not by God's desired role for her spouse to fulfill as her leader. Past experiences with her mate, or awareness of his flaws, causes her to doubt his ability to serve as a leader and offer the security she needs. She often compares her man to other people and still holds onto aspects of her single life instead of cleaving to him as her new family unit.

A venti wifestyle displays prayer, faith, and hope, as she believes her mate can serve as a good leader in their home. While a husband may falter in many ways, a wife can decide to receive him as an authority figure in her life. She lives with added confidence and security because she trusts her spouse as her partner.

Is Your Wifestyle Short or Venti?

Personalize the themes of this chapter by circling the responses that best represent your answer to each question.

	A	B
I prefer to think of my husband as a friend, not an overseer.	True	False
Other husbands may lead their wives, but my guy isn't the leadership type.	True	False
I can cleave to my husband without leaving my parents.	True	False
I tend to appreciate romantic affection more than practical and considerate leadership.	True	False
Please circle words in each column that best describe your recent attitudes or behaviors. Circle all that apply.	Skeptical Defeated Conflicted	Honoring Receptive Trusting

Please tally your results. If you have more "A" answers, those exhibit the habits of a short wifestyle. More "B" answers show a venti wifestyle. Want to receive the blessings of a godly husband? Keep reading!

Ways to Increase Your Portion

Jesus came that we may have life to the full,[13] and this includes abundance in our marriages. Apply these practical steps to receive an increased measure of God's provision through your husband:

- Pay attention to how you react (words, thoughts, attitudes, and actions) the next time your man offers correction or direction. If you don't like your response, talk with God about areas in your heart he wants to heal. If you are emotional in the moment, allow some time to pass, and then approach your husband to discuss ways you both can handle the situation differently to achieve a better outcome in the future.

- Consider the aspects of honor, overcoming conflict, priorities, and economics (HOPE) we discussed in leaving and cleaving. Brainstorm a few ways you can do a better job of building unity with your husband in these areas.

- If it's difficult to view your spouse as a leader in your life, talk with God about it. Ask him to show you *why*. Perhaps it has to do with your experience with other leaders, what you've observed in other couples, or past family or marital wounds. Don't give up. Keep reading; there's good stuff in chapter 3.

- Make intentional choices to include your husband's leadership in your life. Ask him to pray for you. Seek his feedback. Share things you're working through and thank him for acts of love and consideration.

- List ways your spouse sacrifices for you. Include small considerations like taking out the trash, putting gas in the car, or grocery shopping. Don't compare this inventory to your own tasks. This activity will help you pay attention to practical demonstrations of his love.

- Sometimes we see an issue of sin or temptation in our husbands and use that to disqualify their leadership. Don't fall into the trap of judging your mate. Ask the Lord to bring correction and restoration, and to use your husband in your life despite his flaws—that's a prayer God is quick to answer.

What Do You Think?

- How has your man shown a desire to keep you safe physically, emotionally, or spiritually?
- Do you let your spouse offer you security, or do you prefer to stand alone?
- Can you allow your hubby to be your champion without feeling like he's trying to conquer you?
- How has your response to your husband affected your ability to receive his love and leadership?
- Have you redefined love based on your own expectations instead of how God prescribed it to function?

Real Life #Wifestylin: Katie's Story

This testimony came from an Instagram post:

"I've been caught up in negativity, jealously, greed, selfishness, and idolatry. Thankful for a husband who helps me reset my mind on things above. Thankful for the Truth in God's Word, and that he wipes us white as snow. Thankful for forgiveness. From Jesus and others."

Naturally, I had to reach out for the backstory:

December 26, the day after Christmas, I gave into nasty temptation filled with selfishness, discontentment,

---

and complaining over petty issues and unmet expectations. It was ugly. My husband doesn't just come to me with Scripture when I'm in sin. He keeps our marriage Christ-centered in such a way that he helps me meet with Jesus. He leads me, loves me, and reminds me of Scripture, which causes my spirit to be sensitive to God's prompting and conviction. He doesn't usually point out my sin, and the day of this Instagram post, he didn't either. Simply by living his life the way he does, he points me to Jesus. I apologized to him for how I acted and repented to Jesus.

Joey reminds me every time it snows, as it did when I woke up on the 27th (took me a full day to admit my sin), Jesus washes us white as snow. In our marriage, my husband cleanses me and prepares me for holiness by giving me the Word of God in all seasons, the highs, lows, and the normal days. This sets a foundation for repentance and coming to Jesus in the days I need it most.

–Katie Elliott, married in 2012

Notice the beautiful simplicity of this testimony. Katie is able to celebrate the role her husband plays in drawing her closer to Jesus, even, or perhaps especially, when she falters in sin. These gentle reminders help us regain right perspective when circumstances may distract us from the truth

CHAPTER THREE

The *Blessing* of Unity

"For I too am a [woman] under authority . . ."

Matthew 8:9

Some people have music. Others have rhythm. I have neither.

Consider yourself blessed if you've never watched me on the dance floor. Although, what I lack in grace and coordination, I make up for in enthusiasm.

Jared isolates different muscles in his body and picks up cues from tiny musical notes undetected by my untrained ears. He's the smooth to my spaz, the "pop, lock, and drop" to my polka, and waltz to my whimsy. One year, I ignored my clumsy feet and sweaty palms to gift him with a couple's private lesson in ballroom dancing. Here, in the perfect little black dress—it scored a ten in the twirl factor—and strappy heels, I discovered my greatest limitation. I hate to follow his lead.

We received the same direction, knew the teacher, heard the music, and followed the steps. Who said he should be the lead anyway?

Oh. The instructor. The guide we trusted to teach us the way and ensure we had a good time.

> Wives, submit to your own husbands, as to the Lord.
> For the husband is the head of the wife even as Christ
> is the head of the church, his body, and is himself its
> Savior. Now as the church submits to Christ, so also
> wives should submit in everything to their husbands.
> (Eph. 5:22–24)

Remember the part about me needing to follow Jared's steps for our dance to be successful? A tango cannot have two leads, and our Marriage Instructor, our third strand, calls us to submit to our husbands that we may have unity in our relationships and live in concert with his spirit.

Submit

I know *submit* is a fighting word. Instead of warring against it, I ask that for these few minutes together we try to understand submission from a fresh perspective. I'm not asking that we pick up the word and take it home just yet. Ponder it. Watch from a distance as we wander through this chapter, like how you'd eye a stray dog before extending a kind hand. I've come to know that husband-leadership isn't a man-made curse, it's a God-ordained blessing. But you can't take my word for it. Trusting God in marital submission takes understanding beyond what I can give; you need to hear it from him. Consider all you've known . . . witnessed . . . wondered . . . dreaded about the "S" word, and allow yourself to contemplate one simple question: What if true submission something entirely different?

> Husband-leadership isn't a man-made curse, it's a God-ordained blessing.

Not History, HERstory

If you saw pictures from my childhood, say around age five, you wouldn't recognize me. I sported a mullet—it wasn't in style—and my favorite outfit was a bright pink, Minnie Mouse, double-breasted skirt suit. I planned to rule the world, handsome hubby and Barbie dream house included.

I grew up in a neighborhood of boys and trees. I'd throw on messy overalls with faux pearl necklaces to join in berry picking, or race the older kids down hills, and then carpool to the hospital for stitches. The world sparkled as my personal fairy tale, but the glittering storyline grew shabbier with each year—turning more Brothers Grimm than Disney production.

I know few women whose experiences measure up to what they imagined. Where we hoped for abundance, we received short supply.

Guys that refuse to live up to their roles as men.

Leadership by intimidation.

Lack of communication, support, or direction.

Blissful unity in marriage seems a cruel wives' tale, especially when it comes to expressions of authority. The struggle shifts with each generation as we grapple with this submission thing, filtering it through societal norms and cultural adaptations.

Take the Joneses, for example (names changed to protect . . . well . . . everybody). Let's look at three generations of women in one family as they meet up for Sunday brunch, filing into Grandma and Grandpa's house for waffles and pastry sandwiches.

First Generation Wife:
Grandma Dee and Husband Grandpa Dave

Her hair pinned in a silver bun, Grandma Dee's eyes still sparkle with the beauty of youth. Married at a young age to her charismatic army man, Dave, they've loved each other well by anyone's standards. She enjoys the busy hum of a full home, everyone gathered in the kitchen—her domain, especially after quitting her job to raise the kids.

Dave's gruff voice jolts her back into the moment and halts other conversations.

"Cooking has been your only job for the past forty years. You'd think you'd be better at it by now." He bites into a crispy waffle.

Dee notices the awkward silence but pays it no mind as she laughs, "You'd think so, wouldn't you, dear?"

Blunt, but never cruel, Dave has always been the boss in their home. Dee catches her daughter's sympathetic gaze and widens her smile. Linda wishes her mom would stand up to Dave, but Dee knows only to speak when spoken to and keep her opinions to herself. She ignores latent abilities and minor wounds. Her role is to submit, because that's what you do.

Second Generation Wife:
Mom Linda and Husband Larry

Linda sends her mom a knowing smile before shooting a pointed gaze at her own husband, Larry. *My Dad's at it again. Why does he put Mom down this way?*

She cringes with each macho wisecrack and sets about cleaning the kitchen, making every effort to ease Dee's load. Linda's homemaking skills were cultivated with love by her mother, and she feels pride at being the queen of her castle, not relegated to chambermaid—the apparent wifely role in her father's house.

Linda refuses the antiquated oppression her mom calls "submission" and ensures her voice is heard and respected, even feared, in her home. Per usual, she holds her tongue until their car pulls out of her parents' driveway.

"If you are the head of the home, then I am the neck," she resolves.

"You turn me whichever way is best." Larry offers a small nod and monotone refrain, familiar with the monologue. Over the years, he's resigned to keep the peace rather than engage in a constant battle. Linda resolves not to become her mother, but Larry notices a resemblance to her father's overbearing tendencies. Dejected at her lack of respect, he rolls his eyes and turns to stare out the window.

Third Generation Wife:
Daughter Marissa and Husband Michael

Marissa double taps the key fob to unlock the passenger side door as she climbs in the driver's side and slides her legs under the steering wheel. The car ride begins with only the hum of the SUV to score the moment.

"I like our life." Marissa shifts to see Michael better in the passenger seat.

"Me too."

"I think my parents and grandparents are happy, but I don't know that their relationships work. I mean, did you *hear* what Grandpa said? Borderline sexist. And you know Mom took offense; Dad's probably *hearing* about it the whole way home."

"Yep . . . I like your family." Michael winces at his own comment. He wonders if it's wrong to appreciate how Grandma Dee serves Grandpa Dave breakfast even though he's so mean to her. "I especially like your Dad. I feel for him," he adds, grateful Marissa isn't as belittling as her mother.

"Me too. Just don't end up too much like him. I don't think he's really there for Mom emotionally. Grandpa and Grandma have this kind of forced peace in their house, but my parents? It's more like a constant tug-of-war. Talk about a ball and chain to weigh down your relationship."

The silence resumes, heavier than before.

"Tug-of-war?" Michael massages his forehead. "Is that what you think we have, too?"

"Nope." Marissa tucks her hair behind one ear. "We share it. Mutual submission. Sometimes you lead, and sometimes I do." She wiggles playfully in her seat, "We groove together."

"Oh, *that's* what you call it." Michael fidgets, his insides twisting. He's relieved to share the weighty responsibility of leadership in their home but hates how Marissa downplays his role—like he's incapable of leading or caring for their family. This part of their relationship feels so diminishing, but Michael dismisses defensive thoughts and feelings of betrayal. The last thing he wants to do is come across as sexist.

BONUS: Take a closer look at these familial tendencies via a free resource at thejenweaver.com/wifestylebonus

Hindsight gives each new generation a panoramic view of the mistakes made before. So we bob and weave, tuck and pull, trying to fit this awkward thing called submission into our daily lives. Even generational names landmark our transitions; the "Silent" generation, followed by the loud voice of Baby Boomers, the questions of Gen Y, and the cross-collaboration of Gen X in mutual submission.

In this latest trend, we teeter-totter leadership roles as each spouse takes charge with their own hot button projects. But through our decades of shuffling, I find it interesting that no one seems to ask *why*.

Why Submit?

I'm surprised by the similarity in responses when I pose this question to married couples. Antisubmission respondents see "S" as a power play to increase male dominance. Prosubmission advocates provide some semblance of the same answer: "Because God said."

"Wives, submit to your husbands, as is fitting in the Lord" (Col. 3:18) is only part of the story, a small piece of a larger purpose. God doesn't hand out random instructions, and Scripture talks *all over* the place about a wife's responsibility to submit to her husband.[1] So what's the point?

Jesus gives wives submission as a means to grant authority— the blessing of being unified with his purposes and strength. As women, we're *made* for sincere empowerment. When stuff gets real, we get things done, and we change lives forever, with rippling effects for generations. Genuine influence only lasts if it's given, not taken, and the transfer always comes through a hierarchy of order. Being under authority grants us authority, as seen in the story of the Centurion,[2] recounted below with storytelling liberties.

> Genuine influence only lasts if it's given, not taken.

At this time Jesus lives in a fishing village on the Sea of Galilee. He travels the area teaching and healing the sick, so it's no shock that he returns home one day to find a man waiting for a miracle.

What *is* a surprise is the stature of the man, a Roman Centurion with piercing blue eyes. A Gentile named Gerard Butle ... err ... yes, Gerard Butle. Captain of one hundred men, he was promoted through the ranks for his courage, discipline, and skill. He wears full military garb, symbols of his rank and order, and toys with the hilt of his sword as Jesus approaches, eager to ask the Healer to cure his paralyzed servant.

The words tumble out of Gerard's mouth; his sharp jaw and cleft chin tremble with urgency and emotion. Recorded for us in Matthew 8, here's my paraphrase: "I know you are powerful, and I know how power works. I can issue commands because I'm submitted to my overseeing officers, and ultimately, to Caesar. This submission links me to the chain of authority and provides the full backing of the Roman Empire. Jesus, you're submitted to God. So just speak healing, and it will be."

And the Centurion's servant is healed.

As a wife, I also know how power works. The God who holds all authority and all dominion[3] instructs me to submit to my husband as the overseer charged to bring good to my life. If I want to overcome attacks of the enemy,[4] to pray and speak life into my family and ministry, to have my decisions endorsed by the kingdom of Heaven, then I must link to his authority—a chain that flows from God and now, as a wife, through my husband.

Submission means recognizing my spouse as the leader in my home and responding to him as such. Anywhere he has an opportunity to lead, I can yield to his guidance and follow, or refuse his authority and set out on my own. A wife's genuine submission is a volitional attitude, a voluntary heart perspective she chooses for herself—not something her husband can take from her. She must decide that it's more important to live as a team than to have the independence to do what she wants. When she releases a decision, a responsibility, or preference to submit to her mate, "as to the Lord,"[5] her relationship becomes a continuous act of love and worship *unto* God.

> A wife's genuine submission is a volitional attitude, a voluntary heart perspective she chooses for herself.

Jared doesn't police my decisions; I do. I want his covering in how I use my words, time, talent, and energy, so I request his guidance and perspective. I refuse to play tug-of-war for my preferences and instead ask God to give my hubby wisdom as he guides our family. Before I take on a new project, I want his authorization. When I want to serve in a new area, I get his OK—because I want the blessing, unity, and company of his partnership. We seek unanimous decisions, but Jared has the final word and final responsibility before God for what happens to our family.[6] Sure, it's hard when we disagree. But I fight *to* submit. I'd rather reach 10 percent of my dreams but live approved by God than fulfill 90 percent of my passions in resistance to my husband's leadership and, therefore, outside God's favor. Better is one day in his courts than a thousand elsewhere.[7]

Please hear me on this: submission means a yielded heart, not a silenced one. I'm a co-laborer and collaborator with Jared as we seek the Lord and work to prove faithful with his instruction. I have my husband's back, and I trust him to cover me from the front lines.

> Submission means a yielded heart, not a silenced one.

Your man can't consider your feelings if you keep them bottled up inside. Withholding your gifts or insights promotes division, not unity. As you grow as a couple, you'll learn to share conflicting perspectives with respect and how to use unique strengths and abilities to fortify your relationship. If you're talented with numbers, planning, or interior design, then step up in these areas and partner with your spouse to support family goals.

Submission isn't a call to the sidelines. It's the practice of staying woven into your marriage cord. We make hundreds of decisions each day, yet remain submitted through delegated authority. That's the transfer, the opportunity to operate in unity with our husbands for designated responsibilities. The "S" word, the blessing of unity, is a safeguard against unnecessary tasks and from stepping out in independence because we seek our husband's authorization in the what, when, and how to use our strengths.

But that's not how we've always perceived this sacred gift.

Tricked

We've been tricked. Fooled into believing that submission is an aged premise bringing only oppression. The serpent uses the same deceit today as recorded in Genesis.[8]

Did God really say you can't make any decisions by yourself? Are you so less-than?

Paul's message was for a specific period and culture.

A submissive wife is coerced and demeaned by her spouse.

Never mind that Scripture tells us of countless ways the Trinity practices submission in the yielding of authority to one another. Hierarchy is not a product of the Fall; it's an attribute of the Father. The three Persons of God—the Father, Son, and Holy Spirit—show preference and deference to each other.

> How *God* anointed *Jesus* of Nazareth with the *Holy Spirit* and power, and how *he* went around doing good and healing . . . because *God* was with *him*. (Acts 10:38 NIV— emphasis mine)

Jesus is not diminished when he says, "And *I will ask the Father*, and *he will give* you another advocate to help you and be with you forever—*the Spirit* of truth . . ." (John 14:16–17 NIV—emphasis mine), nor when he submits his will to the Father before crucifixion.[9] Christ thrives supernaturally when he operates within the chain of authority. God longs to release his power in our lives, but we must align with his delegation of leadership.

When we believe lies instead, we fight God's freedom and are held captive by a fierce enemy. Debbie Morris says it well in her book *The Blessed Woman*, "When we step out from under our delegated authority, our faith is weakened, our own authority is undermined, and we become open prey for the enemy."[10] I also thank J. Oswald Sanders for his insight,[11] as I found a connection between the plight of the Israelites and how the enemy oppresses wives through false perspectives about submission.

First, Pharaoh offers momentary tastes of freedom to distract from the real purpose—getting out of Egypt. "Go, sacrifice to your God here in the land . . ." (Exod. 8:25 NIV). But what if Moses becomes shortsighted? *A small reprieve would look like immediate success.* Satan perpetuates this lie in our marriages by leading us to believe we can pick and choose areas of submission. *I'll concede on this point but not on others. I agree with him, so I'll submit to his perspective here.* Meanwhile, we are still in the land of captivity, disguising independence by another name.

In Exodus, we find the story of Moses and his journey to lead the Israelites out of slavery in Egypt. After 430 years of captivity, God sends Moses to free his people from their suffering by asking Pharaoh for a three-day holiday.[12] He knows Pharaoh's refusal is the first step toward Israel's freedom, and the plagues begin. With each new affliction, the oppressor's misleading compromises reveal common enemy tactics.

Moses rejects the shallow offer and Pharaoh counters. "I will let you go . . . but you must not go very far" (Exod. 8:28 NIV). The enemy uses this to scare us about outside dangers. *Your husband might get power hungry. What about all those abused women?* As we discussed in the last chapter, submission doesn't apply to abusive leadership or coercion to sin. Jared has never even raised his voice at me. However, when it comes time to submit to his guidance, mis-used authority is an easy excuse. *What about Hitler's wife? Should*

she submit? Like that has anything to do with my clothing budget
. . . and the enemy lures me back into Egypt.

Next, Pharaoh grants permission for only the men to leave,
ensuring they'll return for their belongings and loved ones.[13]
Excluding things from the purview of husband-leadership ensures
our return to captivity. Perhaps it's separate bank accounts, an
unhealthy external relationship, or a past hurt you can't forgive.
These ties hold you captive.

> Excluding things from the purview of husband-
> leadership assures our return to captivity.

Maybe it's through deception that you've been ensnared, a
twisting of God's truth under the guise of *mutual submission*, "submitting to one another out of reverence for Christ" (Eph. 5:21). This
verse is often misunderstood as coleadership in the home, a dance
with two leads. But we can't adapt our definition of submission to
resemble the worldview of a marriage partnership. A creature with
two heads is a monster that goes bump in the night.

Life in Christ does not mirror any earthly culture—Greco-
Roman or present day—it's the culture of heaven. If we continue
reading in Ephesians 5, Paul gives specific instruction on how submission applies to various relationships: for husbands and wives,
children with their parents, and bondservants. He's not suggesting
we take slaves or get married, but provides instruction for submission in various roles. Yet right after telling us to submit to one
another, wives are told to submit *in everything* to their husbands.[14]
So how does that work?

Submission doesn't supersede the order of authority. Just as
Christ doesn't yield to the leadership of the church, the husband
does not yield to the leadership of his wife. Due to the common
misuse of the term *mutual submission,* I prefer to speak of it as

mutual consideration. Mutual consideration is based on God-given roles and responsibilities—the husband as he leads in sacrificial love and the wife as she submits in respect. If we hold to a false promise of *same submission*, our marriages fall out of sync and our lack of unity catapults us back into bondage.

In his final attempt to keep God's children in captivity, the enemy causes despair and discouragement.[15] This crafty serpent touts submission as blind obedience—a silent existence where men are celebrated as big chief and we're little women gathering firewood. He says that we'll lose ourselves and forfeit our strengths to take on our husbands' preferences and ideals. Our adversary invests in these lies because as long as a wife refuses marital submission, she's prevented from receiving authority.

> As long as a wife refuses marital submission, she's prevented from receiving authority.

In moments of panic, we forget the pain we once endured back in Egypt. We forget that God's not just bringing us *out* of something; he's bringing us *into* somewhere. The Promised Land of marital unity means kingdom authority, happiness, and fulfillment as we align with his presence and purpose through our obedience. The Lord guarantees he will listen when we call and will bring us back from captivity,[16] but we must first believe him.

What if my husband is not that leader yet? He has a big head, but it's not sacrificial. I want to wait until Jared is a tip-top leader before I submit, but how can he grow in this capacity if I won't follow? When you let your husband *be the husband* through sacrificial leadership, you strengthen your bond to one another and encourage your individual relationships with God through obedience to his Word. When I rely on my husband to lead, he relies on God to learn how.

And here's the best part. Many times a couple won't move forward with big decisions until they both agree, but even when you can't see eye to eye, you can trust God to take care of you. We're talking about the transfer of *the Lord's* authority, *his* blessing of unity. God honors the wife who honors him.[17]

> The LORD rewards everyone for their righteousness and faithfulness. (1 Sam. 26:23 NIV)

David shares this truth when he spares Saul's life. Even though the king tried to kill him, David refused to retaliate.[18] Independent of convenience and common opinion, he refused to go against the Word of the Lord and believed that God would come through on his behalf. We see this same approach with Abraham, as "his faith and his actions were working together, and his faith was made complete by what he did. . . . 'Abraham believed God, and it was credited to him as righteousness'" (James 2:22–23 NIV).

When we live according to our faith, the Father banks it in our account as righteousness.

> Wives, submit to your own husbands, as to the Lord. (Eph. 5:22)

We don't submit out of reliance on our husbands' wisdom, although trust is valuable. No, we live by faith that God knows what he's doing when he calls us to marital submission. When we choose unity with God over self-preservation, we apply James chapter 2 to our lives as wives:

She was considered righteous for what she did when she submitted to her husband's [budgetary changes / choice of preschool for their daughter / request for better household management / decision to move]. You see that her faith and her actions worked together, and her faith was made complete by what she did. And the Scripture was fulfilled that says, "This woman believed God, and it was credited to her as righteousness."

> BONUS: Download the helpful worksheet
> "Finding Freedom from Enemy Lies" at
> thejenweaver.com/wifestylebonus

Wifestyle: Duel or Dance

The dueling wife lives in a constant power struggle. She'd rather lead her marriage or share the responsibility with her husband. Her efforts are well intentioned, but her reluctance to trust her spouse hinders their relationship. She uses his shortcomings to justify her responses and feels powerless unless she makes the final decision—even if that means waiting until he's convinced to see things her way.

In the dance wifestyle, she changes her speech and actions to encourage her husband's leadership. By accepting her role as an equal yet submissive partner, she no longer vies for his position—a decision that makes room for her husband to learn to lead and love her as Christ designed. As a wife learns to recognize and align with leadership in her marriage, the fruit of her spousal partnership blesses many other areas of her life—including her career and ministry—increasing her authority.

Is Your Wifestyle a Duel or Dance?

Complete this wifestyle quiz to personalize the themes of this chapter in a practical way. Please circle the responses on the next page that best represent your answer to each question.

	A	B
I hate the idea of my husband having the final say in our home.	True	False
I may not leave room for my husband to serve as a leader in our relationship.	True	False
My strong personality or opinions dominate our decision-making process.	True	False
I'm a stronger believer than my husband, so God couldn't want me to submit to him.	True	False
Please circle words in each column that best describe your recent attitudes or behaviors toward your husband. Circle all that apply.	Independent to a fault Judgmental Withdrawn	United Respectful Helpful

Please tally your results. "A" answers exhibit a duel wifestyle. "B" answers show a dance wifestyle. Remember, we all overlap with habits in both wifestyle categories. No matter where we fall in the wifestyle spectrum, we have the chance to think again and choose differently.

Ways to Dance

Unlike your natural fashion sense, no healthy wifestyle is effortless at first. Check out the following ways to grow in the dance wifestyle:

- "We" is the language of unity. Pay attention to your thought and speech patterns to see how often you focus on "me" versus "we." Work on developing consideration for your spouse as you go throughout your day.
- Write out the family responsibilities under your purview. Take this list to your husband, and ask him if he is good with how you manage those things, and what areas he wants to change. Would he rather handle that himself? Or does he have feedback regarding the methods you employ in your management? Be open to what he says. Don't shut down; start a dialogue.

- Create a list of things you'd like to manage for your family and why. If these desires relate to your gifts and abilities, talk with your husband about them. If they're based on a lack of trust or a desire for control, first pray and approach these conversations *not* to ask for the role but to heal that wounded area of your relationship.
- Identify incorrect views of submission and repent to God for them. Then apologize to your husband and share new ways you want to respond to your relationship. This isn't about calling him out to lead; share the practical ways *you* want to submit and come alongside him in unity.
- Submission is not about changing your personality. You can be a strong, outspoken, expressive, passionate woman and still be submitted. You can also be quiet, compliant, and reserved, and *not* live in submission. As you talk with God and your spouse about how to apply these truths to your life, focus on the inward change of your heart and perspectives. As you transform, your actions will follow—refining the beauty of your personality as it flows in line with your faith. Be strong *and* unified.

BONUS: Download worksheets to help you identify and discuss family responsibilities with your husband at thejenweaver.com/wifestylebonus

What Do You Think?
- What lies has the enemy told you about submission to keep you in captivity?
- What areas of comfort in your relationship are familiar bondages, not God-ordained blessings?

- Does God want you to contribute to your family with perspectives or resources you've withheld?
- What truth is God telling you now about the role of submission in your marriage?

Real Life #Wifestylin: Lisa's Story

As my husband, Charles, and I began our life together, there were many times I found myself wondering, "Why doesn't he lead?" Sometimes, I even thought, "I need to lead because I'm stronger than he is." Or "Well, if he won't lead us where we need to go, I will!" While it might have been true that I was spiritually stronger at that time, how was he ever going to BE strong enough? How would he LEARN to lead if I was unwilling to follow? If I truly was stronger in my faith, I should have trusted God to lead the man he had prepared for me. I should have known God's love and Charles's love wouldn't lead us anywhere harmful. This point—trust God wholeheartedly—resonates so strongly with me. I did finally learn that lesson, but my prayer is that the readers of this book will learn it more quickly.

–Lisa, married in 1993

Lisa learned to trust the Lord while her husband learned to lead. She believed God, and he blessed her because of it. But this trust thing is *hard*, especially during difficult seasons or when our men make big mistakes. That's why God gives us the next promise— the blessing of confident assurance in his presence.

CHAPTER FOUR

The *Blessing* of Confident Expectation

"... do not fear anything that is frightening."

1 Peter 3:6

I survived one of those gut-wrenching seasons in my marriage in the months after giving birth to our first child. Jared and I couldn't stay on the same page. We'd reach consensus, then lose our spot before we had the chance to bookmark it, and the lack of sleep didn't help.

I've always been a can-do type person. Internally motivated, others call it. Need something done? Give it to Jen. I love the sense of responsibility, the thrill of a challenge, and my husband came to depend on it. Pre-motherhood, I worked full-time, managed the home, coordinated our ministry involvement, and organized our social lives. We kept those plates spinning and added a baby, with me as the primary caregiver . . . a plan that lasted five minutes before the fine china started crashing. We streamlined and delegated, but with every change I felt the weight of Jared's disappointment.

I asked for childcare two days a week, then three, apologizing for unfolded laundry and empty pantry shelves.

Jared's career advancements required a strenuous work schedule. I tried to catch his falling dinnerware—as was my norm. Somewhere in the middle of unswept floors, cloth diapers, and snoozed Outlook reminders, we kept talking but stopped communicating.

I learned what it felt like to sit in a room with the man you love and feel completely alone.

He was none the wiser.

Our disconnect fed my insecurities as jagged scars from his past . . . my past . . . our past . . . cut fresh wounds in my heart. Guilt became my companion. Guilt for doing some things but not others. Guilt for what didn't get done, for not doing better, not being stronger. Guilty for the guilt, I grew bitter. Jared's capacity seemed limited to his profession when the Jaws of Life forced open my daily functions to include wife, stay at home mom, work from home executive, personal assistant, chef, housekeeper, and somewhere in there, sex kitten. I resented that *we* somehow expected *me* to do everything else.

Oh, and through it all, God talked to me through the pages of this yet unpublished manuscript. About the blessings he wants to give us wives through our husbands and the call to come under their leadership, to live and thrive with confident expectations for the future.

Some days I wanted to curse at my own convictions. It's hard to see God in the tough seasons, and many wives have seen colder winters than I. It seems near impossible to believe the Lord for spousal covering when we stand emotionally naked in the snow.

Even still, here's what I know: I cannot trust God *and* reject what he says. *If* God is good and *if* everything he does is good, *then* submission is good. Recognizing my husband's authority as my leader is good. Obedience to Ephesians 5 is good. To believe otherwise means I doubt God's character. So . . . I choose faith, not fear.

> To believe otherwise means I doubt God's character. So . . . I choose faith, not fear.

Buuut Gawwd

Fear says we must solve a problem too large to handle. It presses down on us, squeezing out every drop of life until we're left like dried flowers—fragile and frozen in time.

Faith says it's not really a problem if God is the solution; it offers confident expectation no matter what obstacles stand in our way.

You may chuckle at my idealized view of the world, but I don't wear rose-colored glasses. Instead I offer Jesus-tinted ones. The privilege of viewing ourselves, our men, and the works of God through the looking glass of the Lord's divinity, not the lens of a sad reality. Fear draws our focus to the harsh existence of how things are. Faith beckons us to the truth of who God is.

For the LORD is good; his steadfast love endures forever,
and his faithfulness to all generations. (Ps. 100:5)

When I carry fear instead of faith, I swap the blessing of confidence for the discouragement of doubt and I approach the Lord with uncertainty. *Buuut Gawwd*, I whine. *Do you realize what you ask of me?*

Buuut Gawwd, this isn't what I expected.

Buuut Gawwd, he doesn't see, doesn't understand, doesn't realize . . .

Living in fear requires no faith. The accuser doesn't make things up; his indictments are justified. I can travel along my married way according to his divisive directions, my eyes peeled for every fault line. And I won't be wrong.

I also won't be able to please God; you need faith for that.[1] My *Buuut Gawwd* list prevents a **But God** shift in my marriage. The Lord waits with patience until I reach the end of my *Buuut Gawwd* complaints. He acknowledges every concern, gently touching each injury. Sometimes I'm trembling by the end. Or angry. But his response never changes. The Lamb of Heaven pulls me into his lap and places my fingers in his nail-scarred hands—a reminder of his divine provision. All hope was lost, **But God** made a way.

> . . . **but God** shows his love for us in that while we were still sinners, Christ died for us. (Rom. 5:8—emphasis mine)

God is not swayed by appearances.[2] If I selected the Lord's spokespeople using my own abilities, I'd look for distinguished leaders, polished orators, established platforms, and well-recognized faces. **But God** went for shepherds.[3] Stutterers.[4] Fishermen.[5] Tax collectors.[6]

> **But God** chose what is foolish in the world to shame the wise; God chose what is weak in the world to shame the strong. (1 Cor. 1:27—emphasis mine)

How I live as a wife is less about my relationship with my husband and more about my relationship with my Savior. Do I trust him to bring his **But God** boldness into a marriage filled with *Buuut Gawwd* concerns?

> How I live as a wife is less about my relationship with my husband and more about my relationship with my Savior.

I know of a woman who dealt with this question in *severe* ways. Her husband carried a grand vision of their family's future but lacked a road map on how to get from point A to B, much less stations X, Y, and Z. Once well established as a family, they became nomads, wandering far from any place she could call home. A businessman, her husband leaned on her good looks and charm to win favor with new associates, sometimes encouraging things to go too far.[7] (Please remember, abuse is never OK.)

If anyone could get a hall pass to ditch faith in favor of fear, I think this wife earned it. But she didn't take the out.

> But let your adorning be the hidden person of the heart with the imperishable beauty of a gentle and quiet spirit, which in God's sight is very precious. For this is how the holy women who hoped in God used to adorn themselves, by submitting to their own husbands, as Sarah obeyed Abraham, calling him lord. And you are her children, if you do good and do not fear anything that is frightening. (1 Pet. 3:4–6)

Sarah's story carries a mature dignity often missing from my life. A holy woman who placed her hope in God's truth despite her circumstances, she stared *what's frightening* in the face and rejected fear. Instead, Sarah walked in the assurance of things hoped for: The surety of the invisible workings of a God she couldn't see. The blessing of confident expectation.

Other than being Abraham's wife, there's little we know about Sarah. We know her name was once Sarai and that she was beautiful and barren. All this time without children, God made promises to Abraham. They'd take walks together, her husband and God, and this man whom she loved always returned with excitement. He was destined as the father of a great nation,[8] his offspring as countless as stars in the night sky.[9]

After one of their visits, when he was ninety-nine years old, Abraham began the excruciating tradition of circumcision, convinced that Sarah would bear the son God promised.[10] Can you imagine the pressure? Hundreds of men enduring an unheard-of procedure as a sign of God's promise that Sarah, a barren woman long past childbearing years, would conceive. If Sarah stared too long at her impossible circumstances, she was sure to receive fear. But notice what she chose instead.

> By faith Sarah herself *received power* to conceive, even when she was past the age, since *she considered him faithful who had promised.* Therefore from one man, and him as good as dead, were born descendants as many as the stars of heaven and as many as the innumerable grains of sand by the seashore. (Heb. 11:11–12—emphasis mine)

God didn't change Sarah's circumstances; he changed her expectations. He didn't roll back the clock to make her young and Abraham testosteronic. He used her faith to deliver his power *despite* her situation. Even with her missteps, doubting laughter, and the mess with her maidservant, the Lord ignored the logic of her *Buuut Gawwd* list and established Sarah as part of the **But God** promise. He displayed faithfulness to Abraham through the faith of his wife. The Lord planted the seed of his promise in her empty womb and added her name to the list of biblical heroes.[11]

> And what more shall I say? For time would fail me to tell of Gideon, Barak, Samson, Jephthah, of David and Samuel and the prophets—who through faith conquered kingdoms, enforced justice, obtained promises, stopped the mouths of lions, quenched the power of fire, escaped the edge of the sword, were made strong out of

weakness, became mighty in war, put foreign armies to flight. (Heb. 11:32–34)

Faith lets us face frightening things without fear. Imagine how Hebrews 11 could read about our lives. By faith, wives carry confident expectation for things yet unseen. For the blessings of godly husbands while our men are still learning to be godly. The salvation of our children and health of our marriages. Healing of broken hearts once smashed to pieces. Freedom to walk under anointed leadership and excel in our callings and giftings. Time would fail me to share every story of your strength in the face of hardship. Your trust in God far outweighs the distrust of this world. Your expectant faith serves as a conduit of God's power—a means to fulfill his promises. As daughters of the King, we are living testaments of who he is.

And that is the crux of the matter.

New Clothes

Perhaps you've heard the story of *The Emperor's New Clothes.* The fabled man paraded around town in his underwear, swindled into believing his clothing was made of something other than nonexistent silk and thread. The royal feared that to admit he couldn't see his imaginary garb would prove him unworthy for his post, disqualified and stupid.

Many of us struggle with similar fears as this mislead monarch, but we've tried solving it with a different approach. To build confidence and prove our worth, we've piled on layer upon layer of tasks and responsibilities. We add societal expectations and familial norms until our foreheads bead with sweat at the compounded weight and heat of it all.

Why, just today, I donned several layers myself. First thing this morning I discarded my PJs for my favorite mom poncho—the one that catches all spills and sneezes. I undid the clasp long enough to put on work clothes underneath. I am, after all, a business professional. At lunch I added active wear. Sporting my public commitment to a healthy lifestyle, I stopped at the grocery store and PO box—because who has time for the gym? Before climbing into bed for the night, I'll add chef hat, crafters apron, housecleaning gloves, BFF bracelets, and Bible study badge. Oh and don't forget that shiny ring on my finger.

I find courage in my layers as I connect with other poncho-apron-running-shorts-clad women. *I can be like you*, my smile screams. *My life is happy too!* And it is happy, even though the next accessory always waits to be had.

Can you relate? Once we've started, we don't dare stop. We feel we must prove our ability, our worth, when beneath our unnecessary and uncomfortable layers, we wear royal garments. Our regal attire remains, plastered to our skin with sweat. Crumpled and forgotten.

Don't get me wrong, I love each activity and cherish their places in my daily life—although I'd ditch the rubber gloves in a heartbeat. My roles and relationships are often God-given. These attributes are part of me but not the defining part. When I rely on what I've done—the niche I carve out for myself in my schedule or home or my role in my marriage—my expectations for happiness rest in the persona I create, not on the one who created me.

Lasting confidence can't come from a sense of self; it must come from an awareness of God. I find myself faced with the question: If I'm not the "I can do it" kerchief-clad-she-hero, who am I? When I let *what I do* define *who I am*, I work to *achieve* my identity instead of *receive* it.

> Lasting confidence can't come from a sense of self; it must come from an awareness of God.

I've even used my marriage to justify my sense of worth. I'll run to the grocery store with dirty hair under a baseball cap, sloppy clothes with dried slobber marks, and galoshes, but make sure to wear my wedding ring so any haters will know that somewhere a man wants all of this.

I ask Jared to help me move a heavy piece of furniture and am quick to remind the room—a.k.a. me, him, our dog, and our toddler—that I could handle it myself if needed. One time he came up behind me, wrapping his arms around my waist as he whispered, "You need me . . . I need you too."

Somehow it's OK for him to call on me but mortifying to need him in return. Like I'm stabbing modern-era womanhood in the back with my lack of self-reliance.

You may find yourself wrestling with this as much as I do. Perhaps as we talk about redefining our roles as wives, you can feel your stomach knotting.

Will I lose myself if I accept this plan for my marriage?

What is my place in all of this? Will I even like it?

The Woman with the Issue

Sometimes we use our failures, not our successes, to define ourselves. I think back to biblical times and how we identify many stories in Scripture not through a person's name but by their unfortunate circumstance.

Man with a demon.

Adulterous woman.

Woman with the issue of blood. First off, that is a horrible nickname. I imagine her getting ready to find Jesus that morning, sadness reflected in her eyes as she identifies with the painful title. The disease makes her unfit for common interaction. Unclean. So while years ago the townspeople knew her name, they now avoid her as *that woman.* The one who bleeds.

She wraps herself up as best she can, taking tender steps with yards of padding—those of us who've birthed children have a clearer picture. She rallies the strength to leave her house and then works to find the courage. For twelve years, she's suffered at the hands of physicians in a world without sterile labs or ultrasounds, spending all she had while her affliction only grew.

She has every reason not to go. Her past warns that it won't work. Her present circumstances caution that she'll be rejected. Her pain shouts that it's not worth it, and her poverty reminds her that all hope is lost. But the bleeding woman "had heard the reports about Jesus"[12] and gained confidence through new expectations.

> For she said, "If I touch even his garments, I will be made well." (Mark 5:28)

Who is she talking to? Unclean, cast out from society, no one else would encourage her to enter such a public place. I believe she speaks faith to herself as she walks from her isolated home on the outskirts of town into the place where Jesus is. With every step, she affirms under her breath, "if I just touch his garments." She moves into the midst of the crowd, careful not to draw attention before she can complete her mission. Get. To. Jesus.

The crowd presses around him, bumping elbows, grabbing his arm. But it was her hand that received his power, a touch motivated by expectant faith.

> He said to her, "Daughter, your faith has made you well; go in peace, and be healed of your disease." (Mark 5:34)

Do you call yourself by an unfortunate nickname? *Unworthy. Forgotten. Misunderstood.* Or could it be that your label sounds promising, but perverts a God-given attribute into a mistaken form of identity? *Self-reliant. Independent.* Maybe you've settled for good enough in your marriage, your perspective limited by past hurts or present afflictions. *Tolerable.* Perhaps your struggles as a wife hinder your relationship, and it's hard to look to God for healing. *Could be worse.* Wherever you find yourself in this moment, let this chapter be your walk into the place where Jesus is. Deposit this good report in your heart.

First came love and his name is Jesus.

See, long before the "first comes love, then comes marriage" checklist, first came love and his name is Jesus. Before we could ever walk down the aisle, make mistakes, or create our task lists, Christ established our worth. The Lord doesn't prescribe to the lay-in-the-bed-you-made philosophy. He calls us into lives of abundance. Our confidence, our sense of self, doesn't come through what we do. It's anchored in *who he is* by what *he's already done.*

> BONUS: Download a beautiful free printable of fifteen ways Jesus identifies you at thejenweaver.com/wifestylebonus

Jared and I have worked through each difficult season in our marriage. Some proved harder, colder, and ickier than others, but each was troublesome in its own way. We found practical application for the themes and tips held within these pages, but nothing renews our relationship more than this truth: It's not about him or me, his problems, my answers, or our shortcomings. It's about getting to Jesus.

I'm tempted to make it about us.

If I could just fix this problem . . . speak my mind . . . get him to understand . . . adjust this circumstance.

If he would just see things from my perspective . . . change this habit . . . love me better . . . revise his approach.

In the stiff frost of our difficult season as new parents, we kept talking until the cold words warmed to genuine communication once again. We listened with humility, each giving of ourselves to better the other. But more vital than our approach to one another, we pressed into Jesus.

If I can just touch his garments.

Christ showed up. Again and again. He came in the middle of the mess, the heartache, and the stress. Little by little, he chipped away at my false sense of identity. He whispered promises to echo against the walls of my heart, pushing out guilt, bitterness, and *Buuut Gawwd* complaints. He built the blessing of confident expectation in my heart, grounded in the truth of his love and presence. And each time he came to my relational winter, he brought a bit of spring with him.

BONUS: Download the "Working through Relationship Winters" worksheet at thejenweaver.com/wifestylebonus

Wifestyle: Doubtful or Decided

The doubtful wife questions if she can trust her husband, because ultimately she's not sure if she trusts God. Her sense of identity and self-worth are tied to her performance—accomplishments or failures—and this includes the role she's taken in her marriage. Circumstances in her home or from other relationships she's seen cause her to operate out of fear and self-preservation rather than expectant faith.

The decided wife finds her confidence and calling in what Jesus says about her. She trusts God for what she does not yet see in her marriage and continually chooses to step out in faith to obey God, believing him for future personal and relational fulfillment. She finds her identity in what the Lord says about her, not in what she does or what society dictates. This wifestyle gives her bold faith, and she watches God move in powerful ways in and through her life.

Is Your Wifestyle Doubtful or Decided?

Let's take this chapter one step further and apply these themes to our own lives. Please circle the responses below that best represent your answer to each question.

	A	B
I receive a sense of identity and self-worth through my role in my marriage and the condition of my spousal relationship.	True	False
I often question God's instruction, even when I know it's him speaking.	True	False
I need to look out for myself; no one else is going to.	True	False
My experiences justify my fears.	True	False
Please circle words in each column that best describe your recent attitudes or behaviors. Circle all that apply.	Pessimistic Fearful Weary	Excited Hopeful Peaceful

Please tally your results. "A" answers correspond to a doubtful wifestyle, and "B" answers to a decided wifestyle. Remember, we are never stuck with our current position on the wifestyle spectrum. God offers you the opportunity to change your experiences as a wife starting right now. *Decide* to live differently!

Ways to Grow as a Decided Wife

Have you decided to receive the identity God destined you for? Here are some practical tips to help you on this journey:

- Ask the Lord to keep talking with you about the role of submission in your marriage. Obeying what he says is easier when we communicate with him through the hard parts of real life application.
- Talk with Jesus about your identity in him. Ask him how he would describe you to his friends. What qualities does the Lord like about you? Ask Jesus to help you see yourself through his eyes and according to his titles, not your own.
- I struggled with guilt and resentment due to the unrealistic expectations Jared and I placed on my role as wife and mom. Be honest with yourself and with your husband about each of your expectations and responsibilities. Talk through your perspectives and find ways to make each other's role a joy, not a burden.
- The next time you make a mistake, use that as an opportunity for God to affirm your identity. Ask him to talk with you, there in the middle of the mess, about his love and his perspective. Nothing you do could change the way God cares for you.
- Apply Hebrews 1 to your interactions with your husband. Approach him with faith, being sure of what you hope for and certain of what you do not see. Ask God to remind you of your husband's role in your life and to help you build faith in how the Lord wants to use him for your good.
- It's OK to be disappointed if things aren't turning out like you hoped. But don't dwell in discouragement. Acknowledge your emotions and ask the Lord to build your faith and hope for the new blessings he will bring to your marriage.

- When fear rises, submit it to the Lord. Don't allow it room in your mind or heart. If helpful, refute your doubts out loud with Scripture.

BONUS: Download the printable "Verses to Combat Fear" at thejenweaver.com/wifestylebonus

What Do You Think?

- Do you see your husband through critical eyes or through Jesus-tinted glasses? What steps can you make today to improve your vision?
- Are your expectations based on God's character and promises or on your circumstances and your own abilities?
- How would you categorize your typical response to your marriage—full of faith or fear?
- How have you seen God provide **But God** answers in the past?
- What items on your *Buuut Gawwd* list does the Lord want you to pray about so he can provide a **But God** answer?

Real Life #Wifestylin: Claire's Story

I am by nature a perfectionist and a control freak, so submission does not come easily. By contrast, my husband is lighthearted and free-spirited.

Early in our marriage, I determined that if I wanted something done quickly and to my high standards I needed to do it myself. Money management, cooking,

---

cleaning, and car maintenance all fell under my juris-diction, and he took charge of planning vacations and any other tasks dealing with entertainment or fun. This seemed like a logical arrangement—I used my strengths and my husband used his. The problem is that I ended up feeling burned out and resentful, and my husband felt powerless and undervalued.

Over the years, as I grew in my relationship with God, I started loosening my grip. I learned to not stress about things I could not control and asked for help when I felt overwhelmed. This was especially true once we had kids. It just wasn't possible for me to do everything myself anymore. Our marriage was good, we were communicating well, but I still found myself stressed out about our finances. I knew how to budget and cut living expenses, but each time I would gain some ground paying back credit cards, a big expense would pull us back underwater. When my husband would ask me why we still had so much debt, I would get upset and defensive. I felt like a failure.

One day I read an article about submission and everything clicked. Our finances suffered because I was not submitting to my husband in that area. I needed him to be more than just passively involved. I needed him to lead our family. Moreover, by taking so much control in this area, I was robbing him of the opportunity to lead.

I immediately sent him an email at work explaining what I had realized. He was on board and eager to get started, so we made plans for a weekend away. I laid everything out on the table, and together we made a plan. We came back home that Sunday with a budget, but also with a clearer understanding of our goals as a family. Since we decided to follow God's plan for our marriage, we have seen nothing but blessings. We realized we had money sitting in an HRA that was available to cover medical bills, our tax return came back as double what we anticipated, and my husband got a small raise. With these unexpected windfalls and following the plan we developed together, we have paid off over $6K of our debt in just three months. However, the most important blessing is that the stress and shame I carried is now gone and we have grown closer as a couple.

–Claire, married in 2004

Coming under her husband's leadership had nothing to do with Claire's inability to handle their budget. She tracked the ledger just fine, but submitting their finances to her spouse and building a financial plan together released God's financial and relational provision in their marriage in a whole new way.

CHAPTER FIVE

The *Blessing* of a Provider

"Enriched in every way to be generous in every way . . ."

2 Corinthians 9:11

Woo-hoo! Girls' movie night! One of the most illustrious times of the year, where calories don't count and we can wear cute PJs without fear of kid spills or nose wipes. Halfway through the movie—romantic comedy, of course—we're camped out on my living room sofa. The day's rough moments fade away as delicious smells of popcorn and chocolate hang in the air, and we're furious at the TV screen. Our heroine's story reached the pivotal make-it-or-break-up moment. Her love requires that she choose between him and her lifelong male BFF, an appalling ultimatum.

We commiserate with the on-screen injustice between mouthfuls of caramel corn and Reese's Pieces. *How dare he? After all she's been through.*

The good guy is the one who wants her to be happy. He'll sacrifice, take less, and let her go if it means she'll be better off. On girls' night we root for him, but in the harsh daylight of tomorrow, he's hardly the one we want to emulate.

Married life is full of choices. How to live. Where to move. What to do. Where to eat. I want Jared's preferences to align with mine. When they differ, I often assume the role of adversary instead of advocate, trusting in my own provision instead of the Lord's.

The Things He Enjoys

As a loving wife, I want Jared to do things he enjoys. Problem is, he picks the wrong things—like wanting to buy a sports car while we're planning to start a family.

Let's rewind a few years, back before our firstborn. We travel as a different family of three—him, me, and Bella, our sweet Honda coupe. Life as a one-car family provides unique adventures and budgetary benefits. Eventually, we add a purring beast of a Chevy Tahoe, but still Jared drives the fast little car. With delightful visions of tiny shoes and baby coos, I advocate for him to upgrade to a family car, a practical sedan for a family of three or four.

My hubby teeters on the edge of practical, and the Car Conundrum of 2012 always stalls in the same place. I picture car seats and snack cups. He imagines hugging the road at high RPMs.

One bright morning, my heart changes. Perhaps it's the happy glow of sunrise, or a good hair day, but whatever the cause, I'm optimistic. If Jared finds a fun car within our budget, why not? We could always sell it later. I text my hubby the happy news, and he returns home that evening with an idea—an older model Nissan 350z.

I imagine grocery shopping with a trunk the size of a duffle bag and hesitate. Costco looms large and out of the question. I share concerns and concede. Even more than the concession, I accept the idea. Excitement spreads on his face as I suggest ways to reorganize the garage to fit his new roadster. I don't stop at tolerating the idea; I'm enthusiastic about it.

Months later, the final trade surpasses all expectations as Jared presents pictures of a different vehicle. One equipped with four doors, incredible reviews, higher horsepower, and a sweet story of the Lord's consideration. A God-wink I'm sure the Lord will remind me of the next time I question God's power or awareness of my needs. On the outside, the story seems rosier because I got my way. But the beauty of the moment came in the way this experience strengthened my relationship with my husband. I didn't back him into a corner, forcing him to choose. I legitimately advocated for what made him happy, and God promoted the best option for our family. This is the blessing of his provision.

> I legitimately advocated for what made him happy, and God promoted the best option for our family.

I forget this lesson when I see my husband as a competitor instead of a leader. Take the following scenarios for example— blunders made by *another woman* who couldn't possibly be me. She just looks like me, goes by my name, and wears my shade of lipstick.

- Our mystery wife keeps a mental tally of her husband's shortcomings so she comes out ahead as the "better" spouse.
- She plays a one-sided game of Who Had It Worse as she recounts the day's catastrophes, airing frustrations to receive sympathy and affirmation. She's even exaggerated moments of hardship to win extra support or "me time" that evening.
- She competes against friends or hobbies for his attention, sometimes feeling frustrated or rejected when he chooses activities that don't include her, and compares his "large" amount of free time to her smaller quantity.

- Her man's historical lack of awareness causes her to make decisions based on her own preferences. She can't trust him to consider her; she has to do it herself.
- She wants her husband to lead but sees his mistakes as disqualifiers. As the official unofficial scorekeeper, she tags herself in as fill-in-family-leader.
- And we can't forget those many little annoying habits . . .

Pet Peeves

I had many pets as a child. Goldfish—the feeder fish kind that live a few days before being replaced by a new one with the same name. Around age five, I got a rat, Jeffrey, named after my baby doll. A few years later, I found two pet rats for sale in a newspaper ad, brothers, who I named Nicky and Alex after the twins on *Full House*. Over time we added a dog and bird, plus a random hamster or two, to the list of household pets. By the time Jared and I met, I had moved out of my parents' home and family pets were faint memories. All but one.

I consider myself a harmonious person, easygoing and gracious. But a few weeks into our relationship, I could tell Jared and my pet Peeves did not get along. So many of Jared's natural tendencies ruffled little Peevie's feathers.

We'd make plans for him to pick me up at 6. Ready at 5:45, I'd often wait until 6:15.

I'm a planner, and for me, making the effort to plan dates is a demonstration of how much you care. Jared lived in the moment, so our dates often began with, "Well, what do you want to do?"

Jared's mental autopilot had a favorite exit in our hometown. The highway split two different ways. No matter where we were headed, we'd take the same exit 95 percent of the time and often circle back to get on the right route again.

Now before you think I'm picking on Jared, please know, I'm really telling on myself. I didn't even like Peeve. He was annoying and cumbersome, getting upset at the littlest issues that someone with my level of maturity (*ahem*) should overlook. But I'd stroke Peeve's little ego. With each misstep, Peevie and I would exchange knowing glances, and I'd feed the pest to keep him quiet. Before long, my little pet grew so large I started to question if Jared and I were a good fit. Thankfully, big stinky peeve showed his face one day when I was talking with a friend at church.

"What about the things that matter?"

Jared was hardworking and kind. Generous. Forgiving. Patient. He loved God and loved people. My pet peeve's squawking couldn't measure up. By focusing on my personal preferences, I almost missed God's perfect provision. Jared wasn't a perfect man, but a perfect match, as our different strengths make up for areas where the other partner lacks.

> By focusing on my personal preferences, I almost missed God's perfect provision.

I'd love to say my pet is long gone, but he still hangs around. Some months he enjoys lavish banquets, prepared by that mystery woman a few pages back. Apparently, I'm not alone, as the Bible includes many warnings about wives with such annoying pests— our ownership proven by our attitudes.

> Better to live in a desert than with a quarrelsome and nagging wife. (Prov. 21:19 NIV)

> Better to live on a corner of the roof than share a house with a quarrelsome wife. (Prov. 25:24 NIV)

As a single woman I could choose if Jared's flaws were reason enough not to commit myself to him for the rest of our lives. Now married, Jared and I are both all in. We're building a life together, and I play a huge role in determining if ours is a home Jared wants to come home to each night.

A Hospitable Home

The verses we read in Proverbs could be summarized this way: it's better to be homeless than to share a home with a combative wife. And here's another one:

> A quarrelsome wife is like the dripping of a leaky roof in
> a rainstorm. (Prov. 27:15 NIV)

Jared and I have faced our fair share of leaky roofs. The trouble goes unnoticed for weeks, sometimes months, as the slow trickle soaks into the wood. A few drops of water are not the problem. It's the continual leaking, accumulating water where it ought not be. The damages increase and grow mold, compromising the structural integrity of the home until the ceiling is spongy to the touch and easily collapsible.

I've noticed Scripture doesn't warn wives about nagging husbands. While I'm sure they exist, I don't think the problem is as prevalent. As women, our brains multitask better, keeping dozens of browser windows and checklists running at the same time. When we look at the men we love, we see the good things and the bad—and a whole bunch of little things that could be "just a little bit better." Nonessentials based on preference.

Abandoning dirty laundry.

Capping the toothpaste.

The way he eats.

Repetitive jokes.

Toilet seat placement.

Leaving a naked toilet paper roll on the holder.

Who does more. Gives more. Listens better. Cares the most.

Whatever shape little pet Peevie takes in your home, you have three options: kick him out, discuss his presence, or feed the beast. How we handle this little pest is often the difference between receiving and rejecting the blessing of God's provision in our marriages.

Kick Him Out

Kick him out of the house. I'm talking about the pet peeve—not your husband. This is the simplest option but not always feasible. Decide it doesn't matter. Pet peeves are *your* problem, not his. You can decide it's not a big enough deal to bother you anymore and let it go. This isn't the same as not wanting to address it, so you hide little Peevie under the rug. He'll soon outgrow his hiding spot, a bigger nuisance than ever.

Discuss His Presence

If a pet peeve is going to hang around, it's worth talking about. The way we handle this conversation is the difference between building your home and tearing it down, and we are wise to tell the difference.[1]

Constructive Communication: "I feel" statements.

Destructive Dripping: "You always/never" statements.

Absolute declarations are not helpful in times of conflict and are usually inaccurate—grievances inflated by our emotions. My husband may tend to run behind schedule, but if he arrived on time even once, he isn't "always" late. Even worse, it puts him on the offensive because I'm pointing a finger at his limitations instead of coming with an open hand to ask for his help with something I struggle with—a.k.a. my minor annoyance.

Constructive Communication: Ask for change.

Destructive Dripping: Demand something different.

Oftentimes, the success of our conversation depends on the approach. Come asking for a change, not demanding it. Even when there's an apparent "best" way—like which way the toilet paper rolls or the best way to get to the grocery store—approach the topic with humility.

Constructive Communication: Address the root issue.

Destructive Dripping: Attacking the action.

Related to the tip above, it's easy to focus on the peeve-worthy action, but this won't fix the problem. Ask questions to understand what motivates his behavior, instead of judging his actions based on how you feel. By learning that Jared took the wrong exit because he was distracted by our conversation, I stopped talking to let him focus for a few minutes before the main turn. I also used this insight in the kitchen when we tried a new recipe, or to pause deep conversations during other tasks—allowing him to focus and preventing avoidable mistakes.

Understanding the cause also includes discovering why it bothers you. Is this triggering a past emotional wound or insecurity?

It's worth noting that often pet peeve issues arise because we're not aware of the *why* behind each other's preferences. You think it's annoying that he absent-mindedly wears the same color shirt every day, but he prefers to allocate brain space to things of greater significance—a habit of a few notable geniuses.

Constructive Communication: The goal is unity.

Destructive Dripping: The goal is quick conformity.

Now we're getting to the root issue. The foundational goal of my pet peeves is conformity; I want Jared to do things my way. Each time he doesn't, it's an affront to my preferences.

> The foundational goal of my pet peeves is conformity; I want him to do things my way.

Instead, I want to aim for unity, a goal that requires mutual agreement. It's not a quick fix, as true harmony is established over time as we change our habits out of preference for one another. By seeking unity with our husbands, we can admit that we may have shortcomings of our own. You, my friend, are a sweet flower, but even a rose comes with some thorns.

BONUS: Download the article "Twelve Healthy Habits of Constructive Communicators" at thejenweaver.com/wifestylebonus

Feed the Beast

If we keep our pet Peeve but pretend he's moved on, Peevie will keep on eating. One day, you'll find your pet monster chewing up your carpet or your furniture—destroying things of value with razor teeth sharpened on issues of insignificance.

Loud Nos and Quiet Yeses

To stop living as competitive and quarrelsome wives, we must change our perspective about provision. I enjoy how *The Message* describes the issue:

> Where do you think all these appalling wars and quarrels come from? Do you think they just happen? Think again. They come about because you want your own way, and fight for it deep inside yourselves . . . You wouldn't think of just asking God for it, would you? And why not? Because you know you'd be asking for what you have no right to. You're spoiled children, each wanting your own way . . . So let God work his will in you. Yell a loud no to the Devil and watch him scamper. Say a quiet

yes to God and he'll be there in no time. . . . (James 4:1–3,
7–8 *The Message*)

We complain because we have not received what we feel entitled
to. So we seek it out ourselves, for our pleasure. In pride, we align
with our own agendas and put ourselves in direct opposition with
the blessings of God.[2] Instead, we can live as those entrusted with
God's supply, not as those entitled to our own expectations.

> We can live as those entrusted with
> God's supply.

The provision of a husband. Your man is part of God's generosity in your life—the human heart to love you like Christ loves the
church.[3] Consider how God cares for you through your husband's
hands—perhaps through financial provision or how he cares for
the kids. Maybe he wages war in prayer, flirts with you to show
affection, or offers emotional stability. Jared often helps me keep
my emotions in check when I overanalyze my insecurities. When
I notice the crazy level rising, I turn to Jared and ask, "Stop freaking out?" Even without knowing the backstory, his response is
the same—a quick, firm, supportive, "Yes, stop freaking out." He
anchors me. Does your hubby do the same?

The good news continues. Ideally, your spouse will jump at the
chance to do you good, and I pray that he does this often. But even
if he falters, he is still part of God's provision. Your man is not the
ultimate provider. God is.

And we know that *God* causes *everything* to work
together for the good of those who love God and are
called according to his purpose for them. (Rom. 8:28 NLT—
emphasis mine)

Do we want to live according to God's provision or our own plans?

When You're Married to an Unbeliever

Some of you face a harder time with this than others because your husband isn't a Christian. Can God really expect you to submit to your husband if he's not submitted to the Lord?

Yes.

Unless your spouse directs you to sin, or abdicates his role through abuse, he is part of God's chain of authority in your life. I'm not going to sugarcoat it—here's the straight-up cold medicine. Things would be easier if you were both believers. Being unequally tied together[4] makes the work harder and the journey difficult. But God has a plan to use you in your husband's life.

The provision of a wife. Check out what it says in 1 Peter 3:

> Wives, in the same way submit yourselves to your own husbands so that, if any of them do not believe the word, they may be won over without words by the behavior of their wives, when they see the purity and reverence of your lives. (1 Pet. 3:1–2 NIV)

Scripture doesn't tell us to take the lead until our husbands come to faith. It gives us hope that our spouses may be won over to the Lord by the way that we live. You are part of God's provision for your man, and if he's not yet a believer, your faith and prayers play a significant part in his salvation story.

Our quiet yeses honor the message of God's love and cover a multitude of sins.[5] I want to make my marriage a home where the best of friends come to live, where my husband sees my daily actions as part of God's goodness in his life.

> A good woman is hard to find, and worth far more than
> diamonds. Her husband trusts her without reserve,
> and never has reason to regret it. Never spiteful, she
> treats him generously all her life long. (Prov. 31:10–12
> *The Message*)

An advocate wife is one of the world's rarest jewels, as her character is forged under great pressure. I wimp out at the challenge when I focus on what I feel entitled to instead of coming with gratitude for what I've been entrusted with.

I deserve romance.

I'm entitled to a husband who considers my wants and needs.

I've earned time to myself.

It's my turn to win.

God entrusts you with his provision. Your expectations may be justified. You are worthy of good things, and the Lord wants to give them to you. But we oppose God when we reject his provision for our own plan. When we advocate for ourselves, we abdicate his blessings. God is not interested in accommodating our selfish desires. The blessing of his provision in our lives and marriages fulfills larger purposes—"enriched in every way to be generous in every way" (2 Cor. 9:11).

> The blessing of God's provision in our lives and marriages fulfills larger purposes.

Each of you should give what you have decided in your heart to give, not reluctantly or under compulsion, for

> God loves a cheerful giver. And God is able to bless
> you abundantly, so that in all things at all times, having
> all that you need, you will abound in every good work.
> (2 Cor. 9:7–8 NIV)

What have you decided in your heart to give to your husband?
"Remember this: Whoever sows sparingly will also reap sparingly, and whoever sows generously will also reap generously"
(2 Cor. 9:6 NIV). When we become advocates for our spouses, we
make room for the King of Heaven to advocate on our behalf.
The farmer sows a few cauliflower seeds and a few plants grow. . . .
Does cauliflower come from seeds? You can tell I'm not a farmer. . . .
The farmer's job is to plant, but God makes it grow.[6] That means
the Lord can make the harvest return to you even if your husband
has no idea. God returns the reward of your cheerful good work.

> Do not be deceived: God cannot be mocked. A man
> reaps what he sows. Whoever sows to please their flesh,
> from the flesh will reap destruction; whoever sows
> to please the Spirit, from the Spirit will reap eternal
> life. Let us not become weary in doing good, for at the
> proper time we will reap a harvest if we do not give up.
> Therefore, as we have opportunity, let us do good to all
> people . . . (Gal. 6:7–10 NIV)

And the Lord's provision is not limited to our marriages. Lack
wisdom? Ask God, and he will answer generously.[7] Seek material
necessities? God knows what we need and will be our supply.[8] He is
our sun and shield, offering favor and honor.[9] The one who can do
abundantly more than we could imagine[10] longs to be our provider.
All he needs is quiet yeses and loud nos.

The Lord's provision is not limited.

Yes to his provision.

No to our self-seeking plans and spousal competition.

Yes to obedience.

No to quarrelsome and nagging tendencies.

Yes to advocating for our husbands instead of for ourselves.

Yes to sowing good seeds, and yes to a good harvest.

Wifestyle: Demand or Supply

The demand wife promotes her own cause and advocates for what she feels is best. She feels betrayed when her spouse wants to take part in activities that don't involve her and doesn't know how to discuss her feelings in a healthy manner. Pet peeves often provoke discord in her relationship because she can't understand why her husband won't avoid the things that annoy her. The demand wife vies for her own preferences and frequently voices her displeasure.

The supply wife promotes her mate's interests and advocates for what makes him happy. She feels gratified at her husband's happiness and is generous toward him with her time and affection. She voices her opinions and hurts to find healing and is constructive in her communication. The supply wife finds her needs satisfied as God upholds her cause and fulfills needs her man may not yet recognize.

Is Your Wifestyle Demand or Supply?

Complete this wifestyle quiz to personalize the themes of this chapter. Please circle the responses below that best represent your answer to each question.

	A	B
I am prone to "destructive dripping" dialogue instead of "constructive communication."	True	False

	A	B
When choosing between my hubby and my pet peeves, Peevie takes priority.	True	False
I compete with my husband, often without his knowledge, and find validation in my victories.	True	False
It frustrates or angers me when I don't get what I feel I'm entitled to in my marriage.	True	False
Please circle words in each column that best describe your recent attitudes or behaviors toward your husband. Circle all that apply.	Punishing Self-advocating Entitled	Generous Spouse-advocating Entrusted

Please tally your results. "A" answers exhibit demand wifestyle tendencies. "B" answers show a supply wifestyle. These quiz results are not titles or judgments—use the insight you receive to align your marital habits with God's instruction. Good consequences will follow.

Ways to Grow as a Supply Wife

Transitioning from a demand wife to a supply wife isn't easy, but it's worth it. Let this verse encourage you as you work through the practical steps and questions on the following pages.

And my God will meet all your needs according to the riches of his glory in Christ Jesus. (Phil. 4:19 NIV)

- Use the tips we discussed in this chapter to talk about past hurts and pet peeves in a constructive way.
- Pray. Ask God to use you to bless your husband, even when he doesn't deserve it—*especially* when he doesn't deserve it.
- Sometimes annoyances come with beautiful silver linings. He forgets to cap the toothpaste in the morning because

he's busy getting the kids ready for school. He gets lost when driving because he's so focused on your conversation. In moments of frustration, train your eyes to focus on the positive, not the negative. Then use this perspective when you speak with your mate: "Honey, I love that you _____. I'd feel [loved/considered/grateful] if you could also _____."

- Talk with God about your needs and ask him to provide you with what he wants for your life. Don't forget to thank the Lord when he comes through!

- If you compete with your husband's external hobbies, consider ways you can join him instead. Maybe you can learn an activity he likes, host game parties, or learn about it to join in conversations as an advocate instead of opponent of his interests.

- When your husband provides for your needs, reinforce these actions by thanking and commending him for them. Even if it feels like the tiniest consideration in a world of missed opportunities, point out that demonstration of love with gratitude. Don't just tell him what he did; share what that action meant to you.

- Work to keep a dialogue open with your husband, especially when you disagree. Offer your perspective without demanding your way, and be open to his insight. He may offer a point of view you hadn't considered.

- If you're married to an unbeliever, please know that God wants to use you as a living testimony for your husband. Consider how your attitude and behavior can show the love of Jesus to your man. I'm not advocating religious manipulation here. Jesus wants to help you live as a genuine advocate for your mate.

What Do You Think?

- What are some of your pet peeves when it comes to your husband?
- Consider your actions and attitudes from the past day or week. Will your husband see recent happenings as demonstrations of God's goodness in his life?
- We reap what we sow. How does what you're reaping during this season in your marriage relate to what you've sown in the past? What new things do you want to plant now for a future harvest?
- Are you advocating for your husband's victory or competing against him?

Real Life #Wifestylin: Kayla's Story

Now I'm not a pet peevish type person, but every item in my kitchen pantry has a home. The spices sit together. The cereals line up on their shelf, and I've designated spots for canned goods, condiments, and vitamins. Any woman who looks at my well-organized pantry can easily see the good sense of it all, but my dear sweet hubby, Marc, doesn't pay attention to its strategic groupings.

He gets up early for work, grabs a multivitamin from the pantry, and returns the bottle to the wrong shelf. When cooking a meal together, basil will somehow end up next to the Cap'n Crunch. I know because I put each item back in its rightful place.

I shouldn't let such a small thing bother me. I'm blessed to have a hubby who wants to make me dinner. He's quick to put groceries away after a shopping trip, and I hate that I'm unhappy with how he does the job.

Well, recently, I spent a whole evening fixing up the pantry. I emptied the shelves, cleaned out all the crumbs, laid shelf liner, and reorganized the dry foods. The thought entered my mind, *I wonder how long until Marc comes and messes this up.* The Holy Spirit immediately corrected me. "I'm not going to let you stress yourself out and create animosity in your marriage over this. Let it go."

So I did. My preference is still there but I've decided it's not worth messing with my relationship or resisting the Holy Spirit. This may sound like such a small issue, but isn't that what pet peeves are after all? By choosing this "little" thing, I'm placing my priorities where they belong.

–Kayla, married in 2010

God cares about the little things. As we see in Kayla's testimony, it's also important to him that we don't let the little things mess with the big things. By adopting a right perspective about this pet peeve issue, Kayla chose to esteem her husband over her preferences and is able to celebrate him for the blessing he is in her life.

CHAPTER SIX

The *Blessing* of Chayil

> "'Many women have done excellently,
> but you surpass them all.'"
>
> *Proverbs 31:29*

A wedding day should come with war paint.

I'm not talking MAC Cosmetics or Urban Decay. Tribal, with bright harsh lines and intricate designs, where each stroke or splash of color demonstrates fierceness.

Wives are not just captivating in beauty and sex appeal. We're women of might.

I think back to the other day and the couple who bought my kitchen table off Craigslist. *Yes, Mom, I was safe about it.* The wife's sweet husband called out as they muscled the cherry wood behemoth to their truck, "You OK, babe?"

Jet-black hair swung in sync with her warrior gait, "I got this. I'm a strong woman." No hesitation.

I wish I lived every part of life with the assuredness of that woman carrying her new table. If your experiences are anything like mine—and we may have some similarities—there's a lot of what I *desire to do* falling outside the reach of what I feel *empowered to do*. Like I'm always playing catch-up. The struggle to "have it all" is real, no matter a woman's age, life path, or social standing.

The Hebrew word *chayil*[1] is biblical—I know, you're shocked, right? It's used in several places in Scripture, but the most familiar locale is in Proverbs 31. The woman we know as "the wife of noble character" is also known as the wife of chayil.

Wait. Don't leave. Every day I find more women who hate that chick for her incomparable achievements. But this passage is a blessing, not a death sentence.

Proverbs 31 isn't a job description; it's a Hebrew acrostic poem. A husband sings these verses to honor his wife and commend her noble deeds in front of their children every Friday night before the Shabbat meal. Somewhere things get messy in translation to the Christian way. Add social media—*Pinterest envy, anyone?*—and so many of us fall over our business-planning-sewing-baking-knitting-working-never-sleeping tables out of complete exhaustion. The nobility of Proverbs 31 is what's often missing from my life. And it's not found by *the doing*.

I don't work with wool and flax. I don't know anyone with a merchant ship, unless you count the cruise ship captain I met on our last vacation, and the farthest I travel for food is the twenty-minute drive to the grocery store. It's the power that matters, not the activity. This Proverbs 31 dame has authority. She is dressed with strength. She considers and perceives and makes wise choices. She's not afraid of things that strike fear in the hearts of others, because her household is covered with *double thickness*.[2] Sure, her physical presentation may include workout pants and a messy bun, but she's clothed with dignity. I imagine her laughing with joy at the prospect of her future. Wisdom falls out of her mouth, and her work speaks for itself. Her kids don't just survive; they overcome. These children commend her, alongside her husband. She oversees well, gives only good, and seeks, works, and thrives with confidence.[3]

If that's the blessing of chayil, sign me up for that. Yes, and please, and thank you. Some for you, too? Double servings over here please, God. Amen.

In the past, I've mistaken this idea of noble character as a nicety, equated to proper etiquette at high tea or amiable charm at the weekly prayer meeting. The definition of chayil shows something different:

- ". . . God who equipped me with *strength* (chayil) and made my way blameless." (Ps. 18:32)
- "With God we will gain the *victory* (chayil), and he will trample down our enemies." (Ps. 60:12 NIV)
- "Shouts of joy and victory resound in the tents of the righteous: 'The LORD's right hand has done *mighty things* (chayil)!'" (Ps. 118:15 NIV)
- "He chose *capable* (chayil) men from all Israel and made them leaders of the people, officials over thousands, hundreds, fifties and tens." (Exod. 18:25 NIV)
- "So Joshua and all the fighting men arose to go up to Ai. And Joshua chose 30,000 mighty men of *valor* (chayil) and sent them out by night." (Josh. 8:3)
- "A wife of *noble character* (chayil) who can find? She is worth far more than rubies." (Prov. 31:10 NIV)

Noble character is a far she-hero cry from what I assumed as a standard for the demure, domesticated goddess. We're warriors—embodying strength and valor, doing mighty things in our families and marriages. As brides, we gain the prestigious role of Official Helper. You are a partner perfectly . . . divinely . . . suited for your husband, endowed with the privilege and opportunity of strength, victory, and virtue.

I'll admit, the title of *helper* once tasted rancid on my tongue. I interpreted it as filling a supporting role in my own life story. I'd read verses like Proverbs 12:4 with disdain: "A wife of noble character is her husband's crown, but a disgraceful wife is like decay in his bones." How dare the Bible equate me to an accessory, an accouterment for my husband's glory?

Then I read Psalm 103, where David praises the Lord for his many benefits, the God who *crowned* him with "steadfast love and mercy."[4] Consider your legacy as a wife of steadfast love. You are a permanent symbol of God's favor upon your husband's head—a noble sign of blessing and authority in your mate's life, not the deterioration of his strength.

The Lord speaks of Israel as a crown of beauty, bright with righteousness. God rejoices over her "as the bridegroom rejoices over the bride." Her new name is "My Delight Is in Her," and her land is named "Married."[5] Welcome to the new land of your marriage! You hold a consecrated designation: no one else is wife to your husband. As such, you define what the word "wife" means to him. Is it a blessing or a curse? Your daily decisions determine if your life is marked by noble purposes, or if you are detoured by unworthy distractions.[6]

Persia's Warrior Princess

I'm not sure why, but "wife of noble character" doesn't have the same ring to me as "wife of mighty valor." The role is the same. I contribute power and strength, and I must fight alongside my husband rather than fight against him.

When reading the story of Esther,[7] I always saw her as victor for the Jews. However, she was also Persia's warrior princess, as she demonstrated chayil for her husband. If any man in the history of the universe didn't deserve a wife of noble character, it was King Xerxes. Here's the scenario, Jen style:

After too many glasses of wine, King Xerxes banishes his wife, Queen Vashti, when she refuses to parade around as his arm candy in front of his friends—palace chatter indicates he wanted her naked, wearing the royal headdress. So now he needs a new queen. Obviously.

As these things tend to go, the king hires a royal matchmaker and dates a lot.

Nope.

Beautiful virgins are *gathered and prepared* for him, like daisies from a field. After 365 days of beauty treatments and cosmetic preparation, Esther catwalks from the harem to the king's chamber. Not anyone's idea of romantic wooing, she finds favor in his . . . um . . . eyes. There's no dreamy proposal story to tell, but an orphaned, exiled Jewish woman is now the queen of Persia.

It's no surprise that Esther's uncle, Mordecai, urges her to keep her heritage a secret, that perhaps God will show divine purpose in her unfortunate circumstances. This proves true when a wicked advisor, Haman—think Persian gangster—tricks the king into declaring genocide against the Jews.

Here's the part we know: Esther fasts, prays, and advocates for her people. She risks her life to seek an audience with the king and sweetens him up with prepared feasts as she shares the truth of her ethnicity. As his wife, Esther had his ear, and she rescues her entire race. Yet, the story is more than that.

Esther proves strong and victorious as a Jew, and also as a wife. She brings to light the deceit and evil intent of her husband's chief advisor and saves him from making a horrible affront to the people of God. Esther is the king's crown, his chayil.

Personally, I would have been antichayil to King Xerxes. My mind already skipped ahead with dozens of ways to solve the problem for the Jewish people. Most of them include assassination attempts, covert ops, and digging tunnels underground. But Esther recognizes her unique position and function in her role as his wife. God uses her for noble purposes *in* and *through* her marriage because she refuses common pitfalls. She doesn't usurp her husband's authority or throw his stupidity in his face. She seeks the Lord and proves her character of greater worth than rubies.[8]

God chose you as your husband's chayil for a specific purpose. You're an intentional crown. Where do you excel while your mate falters? How do you compensate for places he lacks? Let God talk with you about these areas through the next sections of this chapter—not so you can fix him, but to use your strengths to assist where he needs you. Your nobility is not for yourself. You are chayil—the mighty valor—for your husband.

Enabling Grace

The blessing of chayil comes into full effect when we live in God's enabling grace. Different from saving grace, which comes to all who receive salvation, enabling grace empowers you to fulfill God's call on your life. Have you ever felt prompted to do something outside your comfort zone, and the best way to describe the event is that God made a way? The circumstances lined up, and you received provision or unmerited favor as you obeyed the Lord's instruction. That's enabling grace, as when Esther risked her life and went to the king. As a wife, God affords you grace for the tasks he gives you. He empowers you to do good and care for those in your life, and that includes your husband.

But sometimes we become distracted. I am zapped of chayil when I step out of God's enabling grace for my marriage to pursue my agenda. God's grace gives unmerited favor, to make hard things easy. A clear sign I'm taking on tasks I shouldn't is when I reach the end of a day or week in complete exhaustion—not satisfied but tired. Broke tired. I used all my resources and depleted energy reserves.

Sometimes I can name obvious infractions in my attitude—complaining, arguing, or holding onto unresolved conflict. Other times, I step out of grace in momentary choices when I refuse to submit my decisions to counsel. In my life, that means I don't want to hear what Jared has to say.

I know it's pushing my limitations to start another project, but I don't care. *I want to do it anyway.*

I'm pretty sure that this unplanned purchase will exceed the budgetary allotment of funds. *But just a little.*

I abdicate the opportunity to be chayil for my husband when I take on external responsibilities—even acts of kindness or service—without considering how this expenditure of resources and emotional energy will affect my loved ones. The break in our family's chain of authority is never worth it.

BONUS: Not sure you've received saving grace?
Learn how at thejenweaver.com/wifestylebonus

The Role of a Homemaker

A common mistake in is equating wife or chayil with the traditional role of homemaker. Yes, as wives, we are to manage our homes well.[9] Domesticated skills are helpful in this process but not necessary—thank the Lord! When Jared and I married, I knew two dishes: mac and cheese and grilled cheese sandwiches. I still can't iron a shirt without putting in more wrinkles than I'm taking out. But those household activities don't qualify me for the blessing of chayil. The instruction is to manage our homes—so in our family, that meant getting frozen Bertolli meals and a garment steamer.

Consider the illustrious poem of Proverbs 31. The woman is celebrated for her noble deeds, which include *watching* over the affairs of her house and providing portions for her female *servants*.[10] She is commended for using support staff. If you ever use daycare, a babysitter, a housecleaner, an accountant, a personal assistant, or a lawn care guy, can I get an AMEN?! I get things all twisted when I think I must handle everything by myself, or view my purpose as less significant than another's. Stay-at-home moms fulfill a noble calling. So do women called to ministry and the marketplace. The key comes in honoring the flow of authority so that in my management of the home I remain subject to my husband.[11] In different seasons my "home management" has included a monthly housecleaner and childcare. These responsibilities fell under my purview, but I couldn't handle them directly on my own, given other priorities. I came to Jared with the need for additional support, which he approved as the leader in our home and as the one we've agreed will manage our family budget. This freed me up to execute our plan in alignment with our financial goals, releasing me of the burden I carried when trying to handle everything by myself.

This leads me to another key point. I can't submit to my husband's leadership if we don't discuss our needs and expectations—a lesson I learned the hard way. Jared and I dated for a long time—four years—so by the time we wed, I assumed we were already on the same page about . . . everything. But you'll spend your whole lives getting to know your spouse, with each new day providing an opportunity to increase your unity. You both come to the marriage with unspoken and often unrealized expectations about what your lives will look like. Does the occasional cooked meal when you were dating mean dinner every night now that you're wed? You want to stay at home with the kids someday—does your hubby know? Who sleeps on which side of the bed? Unanswered questions like these lead to unnecessary conflict. You can't yield to your husband's leadership, and he can't sacrifice for your preferences, if the two of you don't discuss your individual expectations. Sometimes the chayil you bring to the relationship means initiating the harder conversations, especially for the planning and management of your lives. Pray. Ask the Lord for wisdom and a humble heart. Prepare yourself for these conversations by starting to figure out *what* you want and *why* you want it. Consider how your dreams may impact your family, so your conversation becomes less about "me" and more about "we"—finding what's best for everyone involved. Don't let this stop you from sharing your goals, but acknowledge that the timing or fulfillment of these dreams may need to shift as you consider their impact on your family. This way you'll have an easier time communicating with your husband, and you leave room for him to advocate for your heart's desires, rather than fighting for them yourself.

It's easy to spark arguments, so remember, you're fighting *with* not against your man as you determine what is best for your family together. Use these tips to get started:

- Initiate dialogue before issues escalate, and don't hesitate to hit "pause" and come back to an issue when needed.
- If possible, pick a time when you've both had adequate food and sleep. Jared and I schedule occasional "working date nights," and we both come prepared to discuss difficult subjects while eating good food in distraction-free environments.
- As you develop a plan for your family, keep these conversations private; no court of public opinion is needed. If you reach a roadblock you can't overcome, then seek trusted counsel—with the focus on finding agreement, not winning the argument.

Here are a few areas to consider and discuss:

Familial Expectations. Examine gender-specific roles you each witnessed in your childhood homes, or those you admired in other families. You'll find you've assumed which tasks are "his and hers" in your marriage based on what you've known in the past. In my family, my mom selected home decor and found a spot for it, and my dad would hang it. Jared's mom handled home decorating from start to finish. As a result, we spent the first months of our marriage with framed artwork lining the floors of our apartment and nothing on the walls as we both waited—with minor annoyance—for the other person to do their job.

Career and Educational Goals. What roles do your careers play in your future goals as a family? This can be a touchy conversation, as your individual aspirations cannot take precedence over your commitment to one another. In our family, I've worked a full-time job for our entire marriage. Plus, four months after our wedding, I went back to school for my bachelor's degree. We made these decisions for our future together because my professional success is no longer about me. Naturally, this dialogue and my strenuous schedule led to the next topic—sharing household responsibilities.

Household Responsibilities. Talk with your man about chores and how to consider each other's standards and preferences. My idea of a clean kitchen is about 80 percent of Jared's version. Without that conversation, my efforts always lacked the final 20 percent.

Divvy up cleaning, errands, grocery shopping, and life routines based on your skills and other responsibilities. Also, talk about your expectations for the time for these things to happen. I'd rather have my weekends free for fun activities, so I made the effort to handle my tasks during the week. Jared preferred a lighter load on his workdays, so he saved chores and errands for the weekend. This caused conflict, especially during the years when we shared one vehicle.

Stay fluid in your home management, as you determine together what this looks like for your family in various seasons. Is the split 50/50, 60/40, 90/10, or 5/10 with lots of in-home help? How does that change with your work situations or other life events?

If you experience an inequitable partnership in this area of your marriage, talk about it. I gained lots of personal experience with this one as I struggled to find the balance between life circumstances and my idealized expectations. Both of our moms stayed at home as we grew up, so I felt like I didn't measure up to their example. Never mind that I brought in half our income and went to school full-time. Jared's expectations of home management also came from his childhood, so I didn't meet his standards either. By learning to talk about my perspective in humility and with respect, we found our new normal for mastering the home.

BONUS: Download this helpful article "Thirty Key Home Management Tasks to Talk through with Your Spouse" at thejenweaver.com/wifestylebonus

Seek agreement more than trying to be right or to get your way. Submit your perspectives, and ask that your husband consider you and your suggestions. Remember, even though your home is under your man's leadership, your voice is important and you have valid points to contribute. He should be willing to consider and pray about what you share. If you agree that a task should fall under your purview, learn to do it well. Honor his decisions, and if you don't agree, ask if it can be discussed again at a later time. Two people only walk together for as long as they decide to do so.[12] By honoring my husband with how I manage our home, I remain aligned with God's will and receive God's enabling grace for everything I do. I walk in the blessing of chayil.

Wifestyle: Dangerous or Dame

A wife who devotes her time, attention, and energy to resources outside of God's plan and direction for her life is dangerous to herself, her husband, and her marriage—although she likely doesn't realize it. She finds herself exhausted and frustrated when her hard work yields few results because she invests in responsibilities outside of delegated authority—that which she and her husband have delineated as "his" and "her" responsibilities. A dangerous wife stretches herself too thin and stresses over her lack of resources. She finds herself at constant odds with her husband, using her strength and energy to fight for her ideas rather than use that same energy to contribute to what she knows is most helpful for her marriage.

A dame is the UK title equivalent of a knight. The dame wife goes to battle for her family by fighting alongside her husband. She knows her strengths and her spouse's weaknesses so she can be his perfect complement, attributing might when and where he needs it most. The dame distances herself from lesser acts of complaining and arguing so God can grant her grace for noble purposes in her marriage, such as sharing wisdom and support in humility. Her increased freedom, energy, and resources benefit her marriage and every area of her life as she receives God's enabling grace to fulfill the priorities he gives her. The dame wife seeks her husband's counsel, taking on only the best projects and receiving his help in accomplishing family priorities. By walking in unity and under covering, this dame is free from worry and approaches each task with renewed joy, energy, and excitement.

Does Your Wifestyle Make You Dangerous or a Dame?

Personalize the concepts in this chapter by circling responses that best represent your answer to each question.

	A	B
It's hard for me bring direct support to my husband because I have so many other responsibilities.	True	False
I avoid important conversations or seeking counsel from my spouse because I don't want to hear what he has to say.	True	False
I've perceived being a "helper" as of less value or importance than being a "leader."	True	False
When I consider my responsibilities in the home, I've mostly assumed roles, not received them through discussion and delegation.	True	False
Please circle words in each column that best describe your recent attitudes or behaviors toward your husband. Circle all that apply.	Argumentative Critical Abrasive	Supportive Strengthening Peaceful

Please tally your results. A higher number of "A" answers relates to a dangerous wifestyle. "B" answers correspond to a dame wifestyle. Remember, there is no condemnation. Past or present mistakes don't disqualify you from your future. Respond to what God says to you now and walk in obedience to his direction. He will supply all you need to change this aspect of your life for the better.

Ways to Grow as a Dame Wife

To gain the warrior strength needed for life as a dame wife, I have found it beneficial to focus on a few key areas. Here are a few tips to try:

- Create a list of strengths or abilities you'd like to use to benefit your husband. Then talk with him about them and ask if and how he'd like your support in these areas.

- Ask your man what abilities and strengths he sees in you and how those can support your family. He may have ideas to share, but don't expect an immediate answer. This provides the opportunity for him to ask God for insight or communicate what the Lord has already revealed to him about your unique talents and resourcefulness.

- As you go about your day, ask God to reveal areas where you have taken on responsibilities independent from your husband's leadership. Step back and talk with your mate about these tasks and be open to his guidance, even if it means you must break your commitments to other people or yourself. Be free. You cannot honor God with your service if you dishonor your husband with your participation in things that pass as "acceptable" but not "beneficial." Permissible tasks become detrimental if they hinder your marital partnership.

- Ask the Holy Spirit if there are any things in your life that you need to share with your husband, and follow his direction. A great indicator of something you need to share is the thought, "I don't want to tell him about this." That statement is often a marker of something you shouldn't be doing—whether it's a small embarrassment or intentional step outside his covering. You're sacrificing your chayil. Share that experience and talk through any details as necessary. The situation may seem small, but we must work diligently to prevent secrets from causing division in our marriages.

- Learn how to best communicate with your mate. Consider your tone and word choices; it may be helpful to track common phrases in your marital vocabulary. You'll be surprised by the words that slip or attitudes you convey unknowingly. Work to emulate humility and respect in your dialogue with your husband. Ask him if there are common communication habits that he finds disrespectful.

- Use the information in the "homemaker" section to start meaningful conversations with your hubby on these important topics.

What Do You Think?

- How do you view the role of "helper"?
- In what unique ways are you suited to be your husband's chayil? Have you used your strengths to fight against him, instead of fighting alongside him?
- What attitudes or perspectives hinder your noble role as a wife?
- Are there aspects of your service that communicate pride, not humility? How can you change your approach to show honor to your husband?
- How has this new understanding of Proverbs 31 empowered you to fulfill your role as a wife?

Real Life #Wifestylin: Marianne's Story

When we took personality tests as part of our marriage counseling, our pastor opened the results, studied them for a moment, then leaned back in his chair and took a deep breath. We were polar opposites on nearly every part of the scale.

The pastor later told us this: "Because of your extreme differences, you have the potential to be strong for one another when the other is weak. You

---

have a rare opportunity to be a very complete unit where, between the two of you, nearly every strength is covered because you fill in each other's gaps. But if you don't fill in each other's weaknesses with your oppo-site strengths, you will have a difficult, tension-filled marriage." This has become something we work on every single day because—don't be mistaken—great marriages are hard work. We succeed some of the time, and we fail some of the time. But God's grace always carries us, and I trust my husband to lead us with the love of Christ for the church.

—Marianne, married in 2008

Marianne learned an important lesson about chayil in her premarital counseling sessions. Opposite personalities in a marriage create the potential for conflict and also tremendous strength as you allow love and grace to fortify your relationship. But as we all know, it's easier to understand a concept than to live by it. Don't be discouraged by past disagreements or friction. Wife of mighty valor, today is a new day. Go. Fight. Win.

CHAPTER SEVEN

The *Blessing* of a Good Name

"... Instead, bless–that's your job, to bless.
You'll be a blessing and also get a blessing."

1 Peter 3:9 The Message

Mrs. Weaver.

    Mr. & Mrs. Jared Weaver.

    Mrs. Jennifer Weaver.

    I scrawled the moniker across the pages of my notebook—old enough to know better, yet in love enough not to care. I couldn't wait to take my boyfriend's last name. Ring shopping a good year before he popped the question, every date had me on high alert. And it wasn't all in my head.

    Once I awoke from a nap during an early morning drive to find our car parked at a beach viewpoint and Jared missing. I ventured out to explore and met up with him at the bluff's edge as the sun rose over the ocean. Soaking in the moment, my eyes caught a glimpse of four perfect words scrolled in the sand at the cliff's base.

Will you marry me? I turned to my beloved, my eyes brimming with tears as I watched the color drain from his face. He had set off in search of the restroom, unaware of love's proclamation on the shoreline below.

Never fear—his *actual* proposal came in good time. Full of the love, surprises, and passionate tears I long desired.

Then the work began: The process of becoming one. Of melding our hearts, our homes, and our names. An undertaking that, despite my best intentions, I often sabotage.

The House Is on Fire!

Every wife wants her family name to carry respect, for her husband's reputation to warrant high regard in their local community and group of friends. Yet I've found that instead of learning what R-E-S-P-E-C-T means to our men, and adding to their social stature with our own admiration, many women play the waiting game.

"He hasn't earned it yet."

"Show me a man worth respecting, and I'll give him my respect."

What if a man used a similar qualifier?

"I'll love my wife today if she deserves it."

We'd rally around such a mistreated woman, chasing her husband with tomatoes and tweezers—a.k.a. domesticated torture devices.

Your husband has the privilege and responsibility to drench you with love.

> Each one of you also must love his wife as he loves himself . . . (Eph. 5:33 NIV)

Well, dear friend, please take a gander at your husband. Your role is to respect him.

> . . . and the wife must respect her husband. (Eph. 5:33 NIV)

We can love a person without loving their actions. Esteeming who they are, the value they have in Christ, and the place they hold in our lives and hearts. The same applies to respect. Scripture gives no qualifiers—due regard is warranted by the commitment we make in matrimony. A husband's role automatically merits respect from his wife.

- A wife's *respectful* conduct can win over her spouse when he's not obeying the Word.[1] He hasn't earned any high admiration by his own actions, yet God calls for her respect.
- An elder in the church receives a single serving of honor on the basis of their appointed position—good leader or not. Godly actions garner a *double* portion.[2]

We respond to our husbands with reverence,[3] and they respect us with honor and loving consideration.[4] Neither depends on the actions of the other. He's not the chicken or the egg. Sure, it's easier to respect a husband who does right, just like it's easier to love a wife who's actions are lovable. But external conditions don't excuse either spouse from ignoring the Lord's instruction. Consider how *The Message* translation conveys 1 Peter chapter 3:

> *The same goes for you wives:* Be good wives to your husbands, responsive to their needs. . . .

> *The same goes for you husbands:* Be good husbands to your wives. Honor them, delight in them. . . .

> Summing up: Be agreeable, be sympathetic, be loving, be compassionate, be humble. *That goes for all of you, no exceptions.* No retaliation. No sharp-tongued sarcasm. Instead, bless—that's your job, to bless. You'll be a blessing and also get a blessing.

Whoever wants to embrace life
   and see the day fill up with good,
Here's what you do:
   Say nothing evil or hurtful;
Snub evil and cultivate good;
   run after peace for all you're worth.
God looks on all this with approval,
   listening and responding well to what he's asked.
(1 Pet. 3:1, 7–12 *The Message*—emphasis mine)

What we store in the reservoir of our hearts cascades from the waterfall of our mouths.[5] Often this happens with force and without warning. To wait for a husband's actions to catch up with our expectations postpones the Lord's blessing in our lives.

> What we store in the reservoir of our hearts cascades from the waterfall of our mouths.

When we treat our spouses with respect and honor their roles in our marriages, even when they don't live up to what we feel is their potential, we attract God's gaze of approval. Keep your heart attentive before Jesus.[6] A salt pond cannot produce freshwater,[7] and no man can tame the tongue.[8] This restless taste-bud-studded muscle starts raging fires with just a small spark,[9] and friends, many of us are burning down our own houses when we mean to build them up.[10]

Pay to all what is owed to them: taxes to whom taxes are owed, revenue to whom revenue is owed, respect to whom respect is owed, honor to whom honor is owed. (Rom. 13:7)

Toolboxes

Life and death are in the power of the tongue.[11] The ability to bear up or tear down.

Today, my husband is handy and resourceful around the house. He has patched, installed, built, tightened, replaced, and repaired. Yet he wasn't always dexterous with tools and constructiony things.

In the days approaching our nuptials, we didn't have a screwdriver to our name. Instead, we enlisted my dad for handyman tasks—repaying him with hugs and sweet doe-eyed looks from daughter dearest. At our co-ed wedding shower, some friends gave us the thoughtful present of a starter tool kit, containing all the basic tools a couple would need: hammer, measuring tape, screwdrivers, and duct tape. Thanking them for the thoughtful gift, I followed up my proper etiquette with the most inappropriate display of public dishonor.

Smiling, I leaned over to my soon-to-be husband and quipped, "Yeah, like you know what to do with that."

Our friends chuckled, paying me no mind, but Jared's chin dipped and his eyes fell. After the party, he revealed how much the joke hurt his feelings. When I laughed about his abilities, I discouraged, even dissuaded, his excitement in learning how to maintain our home.

Some might say Jared was too sensitive to a lighthearted jab. I disagree. A wisecrack always carries a grain of truth. Poking fun at this weakness dishonored him on the very day we celebrated his pending leadership in my life. I tarnished his good name in my own heart.

> A wisecrack always carries a grain of truth.

Demeaning talk benefits the speaker, not those who hear it.[12] We ridicule to win the next laugh or to relate to our friends. We've all been in situations where someone's ribbing goes too far and everyone sits in uncomfortable silence until the moment passes. Jared can make fun of himself if he wants, but I refuse to throw my husband under a runaway bus of taunting words. I want him to feel safe with me—vulnerable without fear of his mistakes being trotted out for a laugh at the next dinner party.

Nothing harms a man's credibility more than a corrective wife. She expects him to blow it, sitting in wait for her chance to save the day. I've been there, done that, and bought the bumper sticker.

"No babe, that happened Wednesday, not Friday."

"*He* forgot your gift. Luckily, *I* didn't."

We think of these statements as inconsequential, passing words soon forgotten. But they can plague our men and discredit them to others, because anything we mock relates to an area our men need built up.

A negative mind detracts from a positive life, and a negative mouth discourages a positive lover. The blessing of a good name doesn't mean we make up pretty words or deceive others to make our men appear better than they are. God wants to change what we put in our hearts. To refresh the thoughts we store and perspectives we carry of our husbands. To renew the attitudes of our minds so we honor the work God does in their lives, not detract from it.[13]

BONUS: Download the helpful article "Ten Unintentional Ways a Wife Harms Her Husband's Reputation" at thejenweaver.com/wifestylebonus

As his wife, you're in his head. Two becoming one means your voice now chimes in with his internal self-talk—an inner female spokesperson, reminding him of words and attitudes you've shared before.

| As his wife, you're in his head.

Some men describe their wife's voice as similar to that of the Holy Spirit. Yet other times, internalized voices repeat their greatest fears and failings. As John Eldredge says, men "doubt very much that we have any real strength to offer, and we're pretty certain that if we did offer what we have it wouldn't be enough."[14]

The enemy of our souls plagues our husbands with daily interrogations and accusations. *Who are you to lead or to receive respect? What good could your wife hope to receive from you? You're not so great.* Sometimes my voice reiterates these lies to my husband when, instead of confirming the Lord's calling in his spirit, I set to work on Jared myself.

Fixer Uppers

I love home improvement TV shows—watching hosts take dilapidated eyesores and turn them into dream properties between commercial breaks.

I bring this up now because many wives marry their husbands as fixer uppers. Our God-given nurturing abilities draw us to problems we can fix, and let's be honest, many men are perfect candidates for all-out remodels. But try as we might, our husbands already have a Maker, and God is not taking applications for cocreators in his field. We've all seen shared bylines or television shows with a rolling list of executive producers. The credits in our hubbies' lives are already in print, with no room to add our names as co-contributors. *Created by and set apart for God.*

The Lord creates, depositing his presence, his image, and his purposes, in our lives. Sculpting dust like potter's clay,[15] he breathes life from his being into ours.[16] Each attribute crafted according to his complete vision.

Strengths.

Skills.

Aspects of character and personality.

Opportunities for perseverance and discipline.

I, on the other hand, built a Make-a-Man workshop. I add and subtract stuffing and sparkles, changing his clothes and whispering my preferences into his ear. I don't trust God's blessing of a good name, so I set out to craft my hubby's attributes myself.

"I want this part over here to be different. Let's make him more like me."

If I want to be Cinderella—fancy shoes, new life, fairy-tale dream—I must turn my husband into Prince Charming: smooth rough edges, direct his opinions, and cultivate perspectives better aligned with my own. But God is not a fairy godmother. His transformations don't timeout at midnight. His changes last, while I'm found in the garden gluing wheels to pumpkins and wrestling a footman's uniform onto my miniature pinscher.

> God is not a fairy godmother.

My attempts to mold Jared to the idyllic husband are not only tiring and futile; they're idolatry. My husband is God's creation, crafted in his image.[17] In my zeal to improve—to fix his flaws and shape his actions—I trust my design instead of the Lord's.

> "What profit is an idol when its maker has shaped it, a metal image, a teacher of lies? For its maker trusts in his own creation . . ." (Hab. 2:18)

If I set about fixing my husband, and then trust him as the leader of my family, aren't I just trusting in myself? What good is an overseer if I've worked him over into who and what I want?

I doubt many women set up their husbands as literal gods to worship. Our homes are not littered with candlelit shrines of wedding photos or weird bearded bronze statues. Yet it's idolatry just the same to take the men God created for himself and fashion them according to our preferences.

> Their idols are . . . the work of human hands. They have
> mouths, but do not speak; eyes, but do not see. They
> have hands, but do not feel; feet, but do not walk . . .
> Those who make them become like them; so do all who
> trust in them. (Ps. 115:4–5, 7–8)

Psalm 115 pokes fun at an idol's uselessness. Misguided people craft man-made images as religious gods, manufactured objects unable to function on the human level, much less with divine power.

The world overflows with men of similar limitations.

Silent

- Speechless or unheard because their wives step in with final directives.
- Seeking permission—not collaboration—before making plans.
- It's like pulling teeth to find out what the man wants, feels, or thinks.
- His wife often talks for him—or talks *over* him—in social settings.

Inactive

- He waits for direction instead of taking initiative to see and meet a need.
- His wife removes aspects of family life from his realm of influence or awareness, leaving him highly uninvolved.
- A history of dishwasher reloading / laundry refolding / cooking the "wrong way" discourages him from contributing around the home.
- He responds to decisions with passive indifference.

What a heavy burden to travel through marriage with a man who looks like a husband but doesn't act like it.

My greatest efforts to transform my spouse are worthless. God must carry his work to completion in Jared's heart.[18] How much better to trust the Lord than to put confidence in man![19] See, when I say it with gusto and exclamation points, it almost sounds like I believe it.

But what about confidence in a woman? This one sitting right here. My husband carries a list of things to work on, much of which is in my beautiful handwriting. I rely on my effort to *achieve* a good name instead of walking in the *blessing* of one.

I look at flaws and call them like I see 'em, but when I relinquish my role as cocreator, I make room for the Lord to speak straight to him. Coming to Jared with my wisdom, limited answers, and slanted priorities means the conversation depends on my abilities of persuasion instead of the power of God's conviction. At best, I achieve a temporary result.

> When I relinquish my role as cocreator, I make room for the Lord to speak straight to him.

I'm tired of repping my own name. If Jared was a literal house, he'd have my contractor's sign advertising in the front yard. When I share my perspective with my husband, I don't want the strength of my position to come from eloquent words but from a demonstration of the Spirit's power.[20]

Breaker Overload

Overloading an electrical socket is easy. Plug in the TV, hair dryer, Christmas lights, and refrigerator to the same power strip, and you'll trip the breaker—a safety measure that cuts off power to prevent overheating and electrical fires.

Sweet friends, we tend to overload our men. We mean well, but part of the problem is that we trust our hearts, our heads, and the words of our mouths. The heart is deceitful,[21] the tongue a "world of unrighteousness,"[22] and "there is a way that seems right to a man, but in the end it leads to death."[23]

So what are we to do? Sit back in silence as the world falls apart? No. Watch love build your husband, because knowledge puffs up while love builds up[24] and God is love.[25] If your husband struggles to build a good reputation with you or with others, know that the Lord is not done with him yet, and God is all about changing names.

Jacob, the supplanter, received a blessing and became Israel.[26] From Simon to Peter—and on this rock Jesus built the church.[27] Abram to Abraham,[28] Sarai to Sarah,[29] confirming a promise not yet fulfilled. These name changes came in the midst of transformation, not afterward.

Earth, "a soup of nothingness, a bottomless emptiness . . . God spoke 'Light!' And light appeared."[30] Gideon hid from the Midianites in the winepress and the angel of the Lord greeted him, not with "coward" or "sissy-baby," but as "mighty man of valor."[31] God doesn't look at what man looks at.[32] Otherwise how could he anoint a shepherd as King of Israel?[33] He calls forth what is not, and it becomes. When God speaks of his good promises, I refuse to be distracted by what I don't see, calling my husband by his old name even while God calls out a new thing in his heart.

Instead, I choose the voice of confirmation not condemnation. Celebration, not correction. I ask the Lord to give me gracious eyes, to perceive and contribute to what He is doing in my husband. I don't come with my own construction plans. When I speak, I want my words to carry the Spirit's power,[34] weighty because my heart is alert to the Master's handiwork.

> I choose the voice of confirmation not condemnation. Celebration, not correction.

For years, my eyesight was consumed with my own insight—ways Jared could improve, annoyances I could fix, and habits I could train. For any struggle in his life, I wanted to come with a plan. Workout schedules. Healthy menus. A better budget. A different lifestyle. A new friend. A fresh look. A preferable career.

Now I want to speak prophetically. To speak of what God is doing for Jared's edification, encouragement, and comfort.[35] To catch the faintest scent of God's sweet move and pray it into being for my husband instead of pushing him into it. I want to speak of his growth, not to exhort new changes but to commend him as he responds to the Lord's leading.

I refuse to overload this man with my own plans. I respect God, and I respect the gift of my husband too much to get in their way. No longer the artist looking to refine her work, my role is fun. I'm the attentive observer, noting the strengths and unique undertones of God's masterful craftsmanship. Here in the middle of it all, I get the front row, behind the scenes, up close, and crazy intimate view of holy power at work in one of God's beloved souls. Change produced by the Lord's strength, not my own. The true blessing of a good name.

> Unless the LORD builds the house, those who build it labor in vain. (Ps. 127:1)

Wifestyle: Haughty Eyes or Hottie Eyes

A wife with haughty eyes justifies a lack of respect by focusing on her spouse's flaws and determines to fix him in as many ways as possible. She's exhausted and frustrated by short-lived success but takes every issue as evidence of his need for her guidance. Her husband is put off by her efforts and may withdraw or withhold affection.

A wife with hottie eyes is attractive to God and to her mate by the way she respects her husband and prays for him. She recognizes that God alone is responsible for crafting her man and is intentional in how she approaches his leadership in her marriage. This wife has the potential to fall more in love with her spouse each day as she chooses a gracious perspective, focusing her attention on what God wants to do in her husband and commending his growth instead of fixating on his shortcomings. Through hottie eyes, she watches her mate with happiness as he grows, changes, loves, and thrives in ways that can only be God.

Are Your Wifestyle Eyes Haughty or Hottie?

Complete this wifestyle quiz to personalize the themes of this chapter in a practical way. Please circle the responses below that best represent your answer to each question.

	A	B
My husband doesn't have my respect because he hasn't earned it.	True	False
Sharing embarrassing stories about our men is a way I bond with my friends.	True	False
My husband's recent changes are a product of my effort.	True	False
I speak or share things online without considering how my words may impact my spouse.	True	False
Many areas of conflict in my marriage would be solved if my man learned to consider me.	True	False
Please circle words in each column that best describe your recent attitudes or behaviors toward your husband. Circle all that apply.	Corrective Instructive Poking fun	Commending Encouraging Respectful

Please tally your results. "A" answers exhibit a haughty wifestyle. "B" answers show a hottie wifestyle. Now is the perfect time to take on a new marital outlook!

Ways to Develop Hottie Eyes

Retraining our perspectives takes time. Consider these practical ways to transition your eyes from haughty to hottie:

- Ask the Lord to help guard your heart, because our mouths spill the beans about what we're putting in there.
- Change the question from "Is he worthy of my respect?" to "What would my respect mean to him?" Your attitude and response to your husband can support and exhort him, propelling and compelling him toward what God calls him into.
- Share positive stories in public. Even if you're bursting with anecdotes about his latest blunders, find opportunities instead to talk about his successes or areas of growth—no matter how small.
- If your words to your husband fall on hard soil and nothing grows from the seeds you plant, perhaps you're sowing in the wrong field. Invest in the fields of prayer, patience, encouragement, and grace, and see the harvest the Lord brings about. Thank God in advance for the work he will do in your husband.
- Intentionally encourage your husband once a day. If you notice something good, why not share? Make an effort to express your appreciation for the things he does, no matter how small.
- No one wants to be proved wrong, so we train our eyes to see what we believe. Ask the Lord to help you change your perspective so you're quicker to *believe* and *see* attributes and actions to commend, not correct.

- Write your husband a private note of affirmation, commending the work God is doing in him.
- Speak prophetically about the good things developing in his life. Use phrases like "Wow, you're becoming . . ." or "I see you being/doing/excelling in . . ." to encourage growth in that area. Prophecy in its simplest form is speaking to people for their strengthening, encouragement, and comfort.[36] By acknowledging the seedlings of growth, you speak in advance about the fruit of God's handiwork.
- Participate by sharing your perspective when invited to do so. If you have insight to share, first check your motives. If the *why* is pure, ask the Lord for direction in the *what*, *when*, and *how* to communicate it.

What Do You Think?

- Consider recent words you've spoken to and about your husband. Are they edifying or discouraging?
- Would your husband say that you respect him? If you're brave, ask him!
- Have you trained your eyes to focus on negative or positive aspects of your husband's personality or character?
- Could your husband miss hearing God because he's focusing your on voice instead?

Real Life #Wifestylin: Christie's Story

I met my husband online. I was nineteen years old; he was twenty-three. We talked online for about six months, met, and fell in love. But what did I know of love? I moved in with him and became pregnant at twenty-one. We chose to stick it out together; we

---

chose to fight (and did we ever). He asked me to marry him anyway, and I said yes. My husband didn't know how to be a father. His dad died when he was nine. *How could he know what it meant to be a father when he didn't really have one? How could he know what it meant to be a husband without an example?*

I didn't really have faith growing up, but with a kid of my own, I felt like we should to go to church. My husband wanted nothing to do with it. So then it became my job to make him believe. Every Sunday morning another big fight would ensue. At some point, I stopped going to church because I didn't want to show up alone.

About four years later, God led me to a community of faith, and they held the door open for me. They introduced me to Jesus. I saw how he covered me in grace through all my bad decisions. He loved me through those moments when I didn't love myself.

I met Jesus and, of course, I thought I should introduce my husband to him (apparently I'm not a fast learner). When that didn't take, the enemy started whispering lies. Saying we didn't really love each other and that we wouldn't make it.

Then God spoke to me.

I begged him for direction, truth I couldn't misinterpret. And God showed up through Scripture. "If any woman has a husband who is an unbeliever, and he consents to live with her, she should not divorce him. . . . For how do you know, wife, whether you will save your husband?" (1 Cor. 7:13, 16).

No. This wasn't what I was thinking. But there it was: God's will for my life, for my marriage, for my love. My heart broke open to the truths that had been covered up by the serpent. *How am I reflecting the love of Jesus? How can my husband possibly be made holy and saved if I'm not reflecting the grace-giving, salty tasting, light-bearing, unconditional love of Jesus?*

It's been about four years since that day when Jesus sat down next to me. I know and believe that God is working in my marriage. It's not my job to bring my husband to Christ. My responsibility is to obey Christ, to make my life a reflection of Jesus. And so, yes, it is my cross, but this is also my worship. My husband's faith is his own, and it's growing. I celebrate the teeniest of blessings: when he bows his head to say grace before a meal, when he steps further into fatherhood, when he puts my needs above his own. God has always been with us; I was just looking through fogged up human eyes. And now I finally know what love is.

–Christie, married in 2002

Christie's testimony reads like a love story. It's amazing how Jesus never stopped pursuing her, and even now, he uses her daily demonstrations of love and faith to renew her marriage and woo her husband to himself.

CHAPTER EIGHT

The *Blessing* of Dreams Fulfilled

"But seek first the kingdom of God and his righteousness,
and all these things will be added to you."

Matthew 6:33

According to a certain glass-slippered princess, dreams are wishes your heart makes while your brain is sleeping. I don't mean to call her a liar, but lots of my dreaming happens while I'm awake.

Some are fantasies I can't even hope to come true—like sumptuous chocolate cake that melts fat right off my muffin top. But those tasty daydreams aren't worth talking about here.

Marriage complicates real life aspirations. When, if, and how to pursue my ideal job—whether that's as a corporate executive or stay-at-home mom. Where to live and what accommodations to choose. How to budget for babies, cars, college, and exotic adventures in foreign locales. As with most things in life—and relationships—appropriate actions first begin with establishing the right perspective.

> You cannot build unity with your husband when you're aiming for different visions; eventually your paths will separate.

The blessing of dreams fulfilled starts with a shared common vision. I know that's easier said than done. Sometimes it's like swimming through mud to agree on a restaurant for date night—a problem that thickens into quicksand when planning long-term goals. But a family divided against itself is doomed to fall apart.[1] You cannot build unity with your husband when you're aiming for different visions; eventually your paths will separate.

I encourage you to dream together. I'm not talking formal summit or strategy session, but go ahead and plan one if that floats your tandem kayak.

What does success mean for your relationship?

Where would you both like to see your family in five years? Ten? Twenty-five?

You may uncover secret individual fantasies that don't sync up with your combined vision. Dreams are prickly things. We carry and nurture them, sometimes for years. The risk of losing these precious goals can turn even the best of us into creepy hobbits, defending brass rings at the expense of everything else. As you approach future conversations with your husband, consider the seeds of truth God planted in your heart from earlier chapters. The practical application of God as our third strand, marital unity, confident expectant faith, meekness, and chayil strength is often hardest when planning for our futures. Fight to stay in full accord with your husband. To count his dreams as more significant than your own—not because they are, but because you choose humility and love over ambition and conceit. Look not only to your own interests but also to those of your spouse.[2] Because God is working. In you. Through you. Surrounding you with his will, handiwork, and pleasure.

BONUS: Download a helpful vision planning worksheet at thejenweaver.com/wifestylebonus

Discover

In my super unscientific definition, a dream is anything you hold as a valuable goal for *someday*—a desire that's usually not close enough to be realized or factored into tomorrow's schedule. But it looms in the distance, a glorious snowcapped mountain glistening in the sunlight.

More permanent than passing thoughts or random ideas, dreams carry weight in your spirit. You visualize their fruition, and those images bring happiness. Your spouse deserves to know about anything *that* important to you. To share your joy in future potential, carry the burden in prayer, and allocate resources as you both deem beneficial—the opportunity to work together for the fulfillment of your deepest desires.

I've found most aspirations fall into six main categories:

- Faith (relationships with God, involvement in church, ministry, calling, eternal reward, Sabbath)
- Family (when to have kids, the size of your family, activities and lifestyle, home size/location/type/features, goals for children, emotional well-being)
- Marriage (intimacy, unity, partnership, commitment, shared activities)

- Profession (educational goals, career, calling, promotions, business ownership, dream employers)
- Fun (vacations, traveling, hobbies, bucket list adventures)
- Finances (retirement goals, income, security, lifestyle choices)

> BONUS: Download the article
> "Thirty Questions to Unearth Your Dreams"
> at thejenweaver.com/wifestylebonus

As you think about these headings, start a list of any long-term goals heavy in your heart. These are the desires to entrust to one another, although many of us default to self-advocating instead of entrusting. I rekindle a passion, and it consumes me. My husband doesn't get it. He doesn't understand my mountain. I see excitement and adventure in the snow covered peaks, but to him they sound harsh and cold—nothing like the beach sand and warm rays he imagined. So what's a girl to do?

Let go of the offense. Your husband doesn't mean to offend your dreams. He loves you and wants you to be happy. In this moment, your vision freaks him out. It sounds expensive, outlandish, impossible, and incongruent with the picture he holds for your future together. You can overcome bad first impressions. Prioritize him. Desire God's will for your family—even if that means death to your dream. If necessary, drop the conversation for now, or ask to resume the discussion at a later time. Don't let the potential of what *could be* hinder the here and now of your relationship.

Fight for your dreams . . . in prayer. If you cherish a vision for your future that you can't let go of, bring it to Jesus. Ask him to either take it from you or to bring it into being by *his* power, not yours. Let the Lord win over your husband.

Prioritize what God wants. What I want is never *better* or *more important* than what God wants for me. Some dreams come from the Lord.

Anointed.

Confirmed.

Consecrated.

Others come from me, from nice ideas or fun aspirations—sometimes even random childhood thoughts that I embroidered into my life's treasure map. I don't want to fight God's inspired provision by holding on to an expired daydream. And then there are those good desires—seedlings sent, planted, and watered by the Lord—that still need to be entrusted back to him before they are fulfilled.

Commit

I'm not the natural mothering type. More at home around coffee cups and boardroom meetings, I enjoyed children from afar. I quieted my maternal clock through occasional interactions with Sunday school kids and babysitting favors. When Jared and I first wed, the possibility of ruining children of my own terrified me. We enjoyed three years of life as a married couple before that ticking time bomb went off in my heart. Suddenly, I saw babies everywhere. Tiny shoes, adorable clothes, cute diapers, and even cuter dimpled infant faces.

We sought the Lord together, my sweet husband praying unbiased prayers while I read *What to Expect Before You're Expecting.* (I would have read *What to Expect Before You're Expecting to Be Expecting . . .* if there was such a thing.) After several months, we both felt God's peace and release to get pregnant.

I ran full steam ahead with baby-making plans. Charts, temps, and calendars. Herbs and fertility-boosting foods. Each month Aunt Flow's arrival slapped me in the face, masking period signs as pregnancy symptoms. I'd get up before sunrise to take pregnancy tests, hoping to surprise Jared with positive results, but grateful for the chance to mourn in solitude over another four weeks of deferred dreams.

We conceived after nine months and lost the baby at five weeks gestation. After the year mark, a fertility doctor suggested an IUI—artificial insemination. I would have tried anything, but Jared didn't have peace. That's when I learned that while a dream may *come from* the Lord, it still needs to be *committed* back to him.

It's such a painful place—to carry hope for a promise unfilled, desperate for a good gift that God delivers to all the other houses, but not to you. If you're in a season like this, whether it's wanting children, a career change, a physical move, or spiritual growth, please know you're not alone. God prepares for our prosperous futures,[3] and he wants us to prioritize his presence over our plans.[4]

> God prepares for our prosperous futures, and he wants us to prioritize his presence over our plans.

I didn't give up my dream; I learned to carry it. Holding and waiting to see what God would do, I imagine like the way Mary treasured and pondered the angel's proclamations about Jesus.[5] Jared and I set durations of trying, and then not-trying-but-not-preventing. A designated time for re-evaluation. I committed my dream to the Lord—I didn't want my dreams if they weren't fulfilled by him.

At the right time—much later than I would have liked—Jared received God's peace again. I knew it was the *right time* because of how God moved.

The large out-of-pocket expense became fully covered by insurance.

Praying as I left the doctor's office, the Lord whispered, "I got this," in my spirit.

I knew that whatever the result, it would be good because it was from God.

We found out I was pregnant with Dillon Zane, God's gracious gift born on Thanksgiving Day 2014, three years later than I planned. He is the blessing of a dream fulfilled according to the Lord's perfect purposes.

Choosing Sides

Many times in life, I find myself asking God to be on my side. I pray, "Please bless my plan," instead of "Lord, what is your will?"

I'm reminded of the way God helped Joshua, Moses's personal assistant turned anointed successor. On their journey the Israelites come upon a fortified city. If I were the new guy in charge, I'd hope for a sneak attack, looking for a tiny crack, abandoned gate, or unwatched sewer line. A frontal approach seems much riskier, especially one that relies on weapons of trumpets and footsteps, not catapults or flaming arrows. The victory came because on the seventh day, at the shout of their voices, the "wall fell down flat."[6] The Lord gives them the city after Joshua learns that it's not enough for God to be for *us*. We must be for *him*.

See, before receiving this master plan of walking and loud shouting, Joshua scopes out the enemy, inspecting their wall and wondering about war room preparations within the city gates. He's caught off guard when a man appears before him, the sheen of the stranger's weapon glimmering in the moonlight.

In Jen's version, Joshua unsheathes his sword, heartbeat pounding in his ears as he approaches the man.

"Whose side are you on—ours or our enemies'?"

"Neither. I'm commander of God's army. I've just arrived."[7]

Joshua asks the angel warrior to pick a team, and he's offered the same opportunity.

> Joshua fell, face to the ground, and worshiped. He asked, "What orders does my Master have for his servant?"
> (Josh. 5:14 *The Message*)

That's the blessing of dreams fulfilled. I ask God to be on my side, but the real opportunity is to be on his. He instructs Joshua to "be strong and very courageous, being careful to do according to all the law that Moses my servant commanded you . . . For then you will make your way prosperous, and then you will have good success."[8]

> I ask God to be on my side, but the real opportunity is to be on his.

I like this phrase, "good success." I think of it like *financial prosperity. Rapid promotion. Obedient children. Beautiful jewelry.* But in the original context, the phrase also means "that you may act wisely."

We need strength and courage to follow the Word of the Lord, especially in his instruction for marriage. I want his authority running through my life, in my being and into my activities. But being on God's team in my marriage necessitates that I honor the role my husband is to play. When God tells me to *submit* to Jared. To *honor* and *respect*. Good success and wise actions now add *obedience* to these words.

Jesus taught the disciples to pray for God's kingdom to come, his will to be done on earth *as it is* in heaven.[9] Where he directs, lightning bolts hit their targets.[10] Waves refuse to pass his boundary lines.[11] He sends messengers with his Word, and they arrive without delay. He offers his Son to sacrifice for the world according to his good pleasure.

Seeking first his kingdom puts us on God's side. Each day brings enough worry of its own. But when I prioritize Jesus, he provides *all* I need.[12]

BONUS: Download the article "Finding God's Will in Errands and Housework" at thejenweaver.com/wifestylebonus

Blunders

The most common concern I've heard regarding husbands taking a leadership role in their marriages is not about abuse. It's not even about a lack of love or consideration. The fear boils down to a haunting four-word question:

What if he's wrong?

What if I submit my career choices and I miss out on my dream job?

What if he moves us across the country and the home we buy falls apart?

What if I yield to his final decision and it was the worst possible choice, bankrupting our family, alienating friends, and destroying our relationship?

What if he's never ready to have a baby?

These worrisome questions weigh heavier when they relate to our deepest dreams and goals. But far greater than our risk in following our husbands' leadership is our husbands' risk if they do not do right. Every leader must give an account for those submitted to them.[13] "Therefore whoever resists the authorities resists what God has appointed, and those who resist will incur judgment" (Rom. 13:2).

Submission affords us covering should the cat feces hit the fan. When I submit to God by submitting to my husband, I choose unity. I prioritize God's will over my own and align myself with the authority of heaven.

> Submission affords us covering should the cat feces hit the fan.

Heart Check: Sometimes I call my actions *submissive* when they're really passive aggressive, lazy, or withholding. If I answer "yes" to any of the following questions, I wasn't actually partnering with my husband:

- Did I see my hubby running headlong into a brick wall and look the other way?
- Did I withhold insight out of spite or selfish thinking?
- Am I looking for his permission to do something I know God doesn't want but that I want anyway?
- Did I leave him to figure everything out by himself instead of doing my best to share my perspective with humility and invest in our decision?
- Did I expect him to fail and establish my own backup plan?
- Was I complaining and fighting through every step of compliance?

If I truly submitted to my husband in this area and it blows up like a microwaved hotdog, that's not on me.

Now, what if my husband chooses a wrong path? It's not abusive or leading me to sin, but it wasn't the right choice. Here's what I've learned: if my submission is pure and true, then the mistakes and repercussions are on my man, not me.

Now some of you are thinking, if your husband buys a termite infested shack, you're still there living in it. Maybe so. But when we focus on the circumstance, we miss the big picture blessing. Every good gift is from God.[14] The same God who is able do exceedingly abundantly far more than we could imagine or ask for according to his power at work in us.[15] Who meets all our needs when we seek first his will and his kingdom,[16] adding all the things because we align with his purposes and desires on earth. He blesses those who hear his Word and obey it.[17] "The LORD is good, a stronghold in the day of trouble; he knows those who take refuge in him" (Nah. 1:7).

> Submit yourselves therefore to God. Resist the devil, and he will flee from you. Draw near to God, and he will draw near to you . . . (James 4:7–8)

Our actions always show submission to someone—whether to ourselves, the enemy, or to the Lord. We have the opportunity to partner with our husbands with sincere hearts, as servants of Christ. Yes, we may spend unfortunate days with termites as roommates. But God has our backs, and he always proves faithful. He honors our obedience to his voice. Man may falter, but the Lord is faithful to his promises.[18] He carries the blessing of dreams fulfilled so we can release the responsibility to him with full assurance of faith.

> For God is not unjust so as to overlook your work and the love that you have shown for his name . . . (Heb. 6:10)

Curve Balls

All right, get your glove ready. I'm throwing a curve ball.

Sometimes your husband is responding to the voice of God when he brings you to the home crawling with insects. It's not punishment or revenge for a past mistake. God always works for the good of those who love him.[19]

It's times like this I wish life came with a guidebook. Early chapters made available for your parents to read as they figured out how to care for this fragile perfect little screaming thing they took home from the hospital. As the years pass, the handbook could go with you to school, helping you navigate bullies, cliques, and broken BFF bracelets—a trusty playbook guiding us away from painful broken hearts and poor fashion choices. If there was such a thing, we'd whip out our trusty directories in this season of life, finding timelines for milestones like diplomas, home purchases, promotions, and when to start stocking diapers.

In the Lord's wisdom, he doesn't offer such manuals. We'd ditch so many of his plans if we saw them coming.

Imagine David, a ruddy youth with beautiful eyes.[20] This teen is out in the field with the family sheep when he notices the section labeled "King of Israel" in his life's table of contents. Intrigued, he flips through the pages to discover years of future hardship. King Saul's jealousy and attempts on his life, an enemy for the rest of his days.[21] Years on the run, living in caves, hiding from an adversary he refuses to harm. Think David may have reconsidered Samuel's anointing?

Or consider Joseph.[22] Hated by his brothers, they sell him into slavery. His master's wife avails herself to him, and upset by his refusal, she gets him imprisoned. He interprets dreams for the cupbearer and baker during their stint, and the cupbearer forgets about him until Pharaoh has another dream *two years* later.

But listen to Joseph's perspective when he speaks again to his slave trading brothers: "It was not you who sent me here, but God . . ." (Gen. 45:8). "You meant evil against me, but God meant it for good . . ." (Gen. 50:20). We may look at the result, second in command to Pharaoh, saving Egypt and his family from famine, and see that as the *good* God intended. But we'd miss the sweetest sticky parts—how the Lord showed himself to Joseph and prospered him in the middle of difficulty.

> The LORD was with Joseph, and he became a successful man, and he was in the house of his Egyptian master. His master saw that the LORD was with him and that the LORD caused all that he did to succeed in his hands. So Joseph found favor in his sight and attended him . . . the LORD blessed the Egyptian's house for Joseph's sake . . . (Gen. 39:2–5)

> The LORD was with Joseph and showed him steadfast love and gave him favor in the sight of the keeper of the prison . . . And whatever he did, the LORD made it succeed. (Gen. 39:21, 23)

What if those "wiser choices" we advocate are based on man's wisdom, not God's power? The less-than-pleasant circumstances we experience may be a sign of the Lord's faithfulness, not our husbands' folly. Sometimes I am quick to judge, assuming today's issues prove I can't trust my husband to lead; in reality, they may prove the opposite.

> The less-than-pleasant circumstances we experience may be a sign of the Lord's faithfulness, not our husbands' folly.

And even still, say your man was wrong. Horribly excruciatingly erroneous. God fulfills his promises by blessing icky situations with incredible miracles. The stupidest mistakes we can imagine can stand redeemed by our loving Heavenly Father . . . if we leave him room to work.

As a teen, I went to a few Christian dances, and the chaperones at those things had a favorite saying. They'd walk up to a couple cuddling or hip swaying together and stick the Good Book between them.

"Bible width apart. Leave room for the Holy Spirit."

How they determined that the Spirit was only as big as an NIV leather bound, I have no idea. But the phrase keeps ringing in my head.

Our marriages need room for the Holy Spirit.

As we discussed earlier, the Spirit is our teacher, our reminder and guide into truth. But sometimes I want to assume that role for my mate—especially when we're talking about one of my dreams.

Both bedfellows have the opportunity to commit their ways to the Lord and trust him to act. When we delight ourselves in God, he gives us the desires of our hearts.[23] But Psalm 37 and the blessing of dreams fulfilled aren't promises of a Bentley bonus. As we draw near to God, our hearts become more like his, and he gives us the dreams and desires that deserve room there—purposes aligned with his spirit.

If your husband isn't as strong in his faith, give him a chance to work out. Faith is a muscle, and it only grows when it's used. Encourage him to talk with God and to become familiar with his voice. Continue seeking the Lord for yourself, but don't use your relationship with God to dominate your man's connection with the Father.

> Faith is a muscle, and it only grows when it's used.

Imagine the Holy Spirit like a houseguest. If every time your hubby asked a question, you curtailed the answer, how would your man ever get to know him for himself?

"Holy Spirit and I were talking about this earlier and he said to me . . ."

Yes, seek the Lord. But don't use his presence in your life to replace the Spirit's guidance in your husband's heart. God wants to be found by *both of you*.[24] Make room for God's direction in your life, your marriage, and in the fulfillment of your dreams. You may be surprised by the fruitfulness he brings and the creative ways he sets you up as spousal allies instead of solo soldiers.

A Call to Arms

As husband and wife, we fight for one another's dreams as armor bearers—wartime partners who stand firm in great danger, carrying shields and blades to aid their champions in the attack. They stay close at hand, often killing wounded enemy fighters. These warriors don't watch from the sidelines; they get their hands dirty in the thick of battle.

One day, in the real life occurrences of 1 Samuel 14, the Israelites were again at odds with the Philistines. Without alerting his father, or any of their six hundred soldiers, Prince Jonathan heads off with his armor bearer and launches an attack.

They approach the pass to the Philistine garrison, flanked by steep cliffs on either side. Adrenaline and pure gumption surging through his veins, Jonathan turns to his armor bearer: "Let's get these jerks." (Jen's paraphrase, remember.) "Maybe God will do something."

Right there, with the *maybe*, that's where I'd have some questions as Jonathan's best armor buddy. But not this guy—nope, he was all in.

"Go ahead. Do what you think best. I'm with you all the way."
So Jonathan devises a foolproof plan.

> "Here's what we'll do. We'll cross over the pass and let
> the men see we're there. If they say, 'Halt! Don't move
> until we check you out,' we'll stay put and not go up. But
> if they say, 'Come on up,' we'll go right up—and we'll
> know God has given them to us. That will be our sign."
> (1 Sam. 14:8–10 *The Message*)

And it worked.

> Jonathan scrambled up on all fours, his armor bearer
> right on his heels. When the Philistines came running
> up to them, he knocked them flat, his armor bearer right
> behind finishing them off, bashing their heads in with
> stones. In this first bloody encounter, Jonathan and his
> armor bearer killed about twenty men. That set off a
> terrific upheaval in both camp and field, the soldiers in
> the garrison and the raiding squad badly shaken up, the
> ground itself shuddering—panic like you've never seen
> before! (1 Sam. 14:13–15 *The Message*)

The role of an armor bearer isn't about leadership; it's about partnership. Each of you faces your own battles. His passion. Your ministry. An area of perseverance or character development. You get to fight alongside one another. One of you advances and the other wields weapons of support—a starter and finisher, shaking up the enemy camp as you forge ahead in the calling God placed on your lives.

> Living and collaborating as warriors along-
> side our husbands requires communication
> and coordination.

Armor bearers must be present to be of benefit. They can't be off doing their own thing, fighting separate battles while their teammate heads into combat. Living and collaborating as warriors alongside our husbands requires communication and coordination. We must choose to be there for one another. To advocate for each other's dreams and combine resources to make huge advances, trusting God to guide our steps in the blessing of dreams fulfilled.

Wifestyle: MVP or Dream Team

The MVP wife is the best player on her team, and she knows it. She struggles to entrust her dreams to her husband for fear that he won't understand, won't agree, or will mess things up. As the MVP, she uses difficult circumstances or past mistakes to justify why she shouldn't follow his leadership. When he shares his goals, she has the tendency to take over to make them happen, and she grows impatient waiting for him to grow in faith or in his ability to hear God speak.

The Dream Team wife recognizes the value of her marriage partnership. She thrives as a confidant, carrying her husband's dreams, praying for them, and contributing resources to support progress at his request. She encourages her spouse to receive direction from God for their family and trusts him with the secret wishes of her heart. As part of the Dream Team, this couple contributes strength and resources to one another, advocating for each other's happiness.

Is Your Wifestyle MVP or Dream Team?

Complete this wifestyle quiz to examine this chapter in a practical way. Please circle the responses that best represent your answer to each question.

	A	B
Many of my dreams for our family are based on what I want, not on what we've decided together.	True	False
When my husband shares his dreams, I step in to coach him along in their fulfillment.	True	False
I want God to give me permission for my goals instead of seeking to receive his vision for my life.	True	False
I use difficult circumstances to justify why my husband isn't qualified as a leader.	True	False
Based on how I spend my time, it seems my personal dreams are my top priority.	True	False
Please circle words in each column that best describe your recent attitudes or behaviors toward your husband. Circle all that apply.	Combative Coaching Overbearing	Intimate Collaborator Unified

Please tally your results. If you have more "A" answers, you're exhibiting a MVP wifestyle. "B" answers show a Dream Team wifestyle.

Ways to Develop a Dream Team Wifestyle

Ready to be part of a dream team? Consider implementing these action items as you build that winning team spirit:

- Create a joint vision with your husband. Talk about each of your plans for your lives and your marriage. As your husband shares his goals, support the desires of his heart without jumping in to take the lead. Concerned you may overstep? Ask him.
- The next time your hubby comes to share something with you, seek to understand more than to agree or disagree.

Affirm what's in his heart. Relate to what he's going through, and you may be surprised with how much more he shares.

- *Ask* if he wants your advice before offering it. If you feel an urgent need to voice your perspectives, come with humble requests, not demands. "I have some concerns I'd like to discuss."

- Pray for God to direct and bless his goals. Favor. Open doors. Growth and personal development. Humility. Bring his dreams before the Lord in prayer instead of trying to hurry their fruition, especially if he's not very motivated. Ask the Lord to plant passions and hopes deep within his spirit.

- Encourage your husband to seek the Lord more than he seeks insight from you. The dream team wifestyle is about how you respond *while* your husband becomes a leader. The *after* part is easier, when he leads and loves well—which is a continual process, not final destination. We prove our character in the *before* and *during* seasons of development.

- Schedule dates to discuss important topics. If you don't agree on a significant decision, find a calm stopping point and let the issue rest there until a later conversation. Better to be unified on an extended timeline than to run "on time" but with discord.

- Sometimes we can be too quick to rely on our own wisdom or initial reactions. Prove yourself trustworthy by seeking God's wisdom.

What Do You Think?

- Do you coach or treasure your husband's future hopes?

- If your man hesitates to share with you, could any of that reluctance come from past experiences with you as coach?
- As you consider the plans heavy on your heart today, have you committed those desires to the Lord?
- How will advocating and praying for your man's dreams change your relationship?

Real Life #Wifestylin: Kristen's Story

After being in ministry for ten years, my husband, Zach, and I both felt it was time to step down and focus on entrepreneurial ideas. We were drowning in student loan debt and desperate to be free from it. For two years, we strived to make our businesses happen, but no matter what we did, things just weren't working. We hit really hard times and grew bitter toward God. My striving came to an abrupt halt when I went away to a conference, expecting to learn how to grow my business. Instead, God reminded me what I was called to do, and for the first time, I saw things clearly. He showed me that Zach and I had walked dangerously far from our callings and that we need to return to him. When I got home, I began the process of shutting down my business and told Zach that he needed to do the same. I told him we were supposed to be in ministry and that we needed to drop everything we'd worked for. I don't know why I expected him to welcome that with open arms, but he was not on board. It was as if a brick wall had been built between us. For the first time in our relationship, we were not on the same page. So of course, I kept bringing it up, nagging him, telling him he needed to pray, and begging him to see what I saw. I was relentless. After a week or so, a wise friend gently told me to shut up and just pray for my husband. So I did. I encouraged him once more to pray about what I'd said, and I bit my tongue and prayed from a distance.

It was **hard**. Everything felt uncertain. I thought of friends whose marriages fell apart in similar circumstances, and I was terrified that ours would too. In spite of my fears, I waited for God to speak to my husband's heart. After a few weeks of silent prayers, Zach told me he was quitting his job and that he sensed God leading us back into ministry. I wish I could describe the wonderful feeling of being in sync with each other and with God again. We entered a sweet season of prayer and anticipation. Six weeks after he quit his job, Zach began the process of accepting a full-time ministry position. The Holy Spirit is a far greater convincer than I could ever hope to be. I struggled to keep my thoughts to myself, but it was worth it to see the Holy Spirit work in my husband's life. He is thriving in his new ministry and leading our family with wisdom and confidence. I know I could have dragged him along and eventually convinced him to go back into ministry on my own, but to what end? Just to repeat the process months or years later? He needed to wrestle with the Holy Spirit, not his wife, and I needed to respect that process. Facing a relational brick wall, I had to step back and let the Holy Spirit do what he does best. It's the best thing I've ever done for my marriage, and I can promise you will never regret letting the Holy Spirit work without interruption.

—*Kristen LaValley, married in 2008 (kristenlavalley.com)*

Kristen heard the Lord. She knew it. God knew it. But the Holy Spirit still needed to communicate with her husband, to plant dreams for their future in Zach's heart. By stepping back and lifting their situation to the Lord in prayer, Kristen committed their future to him and watched God's divine power at work.

CHAPTER NINE

The *Blessing* of a Safe Haven

"Be kind to one another, tenderhearted,
forgiving one another, as God in Christ forgave you."

Ephesians 4:32

I feel safest with Jared's arms around me. With my back pressed to his chest, his arms engulf mine, and I melt into the warmth of his heartbeat. Our breath synchronizes—the natural by-product of an exhale means we inhale together. We catch these moments with ease, like stepping from shadows into sunlight. But staying, loving, living in this secure rhythm requires effort.

Safety often takes center stage in my marriage daydreams. I want my relationship to carry the comfort of a blanket fort and the security of a fortress. For our love to offer sanctuary when the world gets crazy, blessing us with a marital safe haven. But running here and there, tackling this project, that relationship. His thing. My thing. Our kid thing. Somehow all this peels away that layer of insulation, making our home a drive-through pit stop instead of a place of rest.

> I want my relationship to carry the comfort of a blanket fort and the security of a fortress.

If life runs on military strategy and meticulous timetables, there's no room to grow into our roles. No space to make mistakes or handle hurt feelings. Always hurried, I depend on precision and accuracy, so I sacrifice *grace* for *achievement, peacemaking* for *peacekeeping*, and trade *safe* for *tame*.

The problem with a docile marriage is that it's . . . broken. The will to thrive has gone out of it. We've missed the point if we dive into these pages and emerge with gender stereotypes. Marriage is designed to overflow with vibrant color. The comingling of fierce faith and love and hope. A shielded refuge where husbands and wives learn and grow without the threat of annihilation. That's the blessing of a safe haven.

Marriage, like life, is never mild for long. It's full of twists and turns, soaring highs and swooping lows that make your stomach twirl before it drops. The connections we have with our husbands change with time. What is weakened by circumstance can be strengthened by choice.

We describe spousal relationships with candy-coated words, and these phrases become . . . benign. Agreeable in a harmless balmy kind of way. Pleasant, not powerful.

Marriage means forgiving.

It's fun. Romantic. Uplifting.

Life with sugared niceties, these common phrases can be dangerously misleading if we speak the words without considering what they mean. These qualities . . . experiences . . . priorities—they carry weight. Substance. The oomph that keeps us weathering the storms instead of abandoning our relationship. Far from a sprint or stroll, marriage is a marathon—complete with long stretches and moments in desperate need of refreshment.

Marathon runner finds its place on the list of things I am *not*. But even as an occasional 5K'er, I know I won't make it fifty feet if I haven't decided to do so. I may show up to the race wearing fun themed attire. I can stretch and hydrate with the best of them, but if I'm already wishing I could stop before we start, I will not make it far.

When my internal—or external—voice echoes with each step, "I want to stop . . . I hate running . . . why did I do this . . ." I'm not going to finish. I lose the will to run. I quit even faster if my cheering section becomes a pessimistic peanut gallery. Instead of holding glittery signs and offering tiny cold beverages, they pull up lounge chairs and call for me to join them.

"Boo! You're wasting your time."

Marriage is harder than running a marathon, I imagine. The security of our relationships comes not in nice quiet afternoons but down in the mess of it all. When we pull back the curtain on our smooth seas to reveal rip tides and undercurrents—and we refuse to let things stay that way.

What we do when faced with the crazy—that's what makes a marriage last.

If we give in or conquer.

Fight for or against.

Press in or push away.

Build a safe haven or tear away at our walls of security.

Even in the worst argument or lowest moment, I refuse to bring *divorce* into my relationship vocabulary. I've heard women say, "If my husband does _____, I'd leave him." The enemy can hear her words too, and she gives him the key to destruction.

Please know, my friends, I don't come with judgment or condemnation, but encouragement. We're part of a royal priesthood.[1]
A chosen people to declare God's praises. We approach him with
confidence because the one who sits on the throne sympathizes
with our weaknesses, offering mercy and grace for our times of
need.[2]

Sometimes I view my husband through a lesser hope. While
Jesus is out doing his saving, healing, forgiving, grace-filled thing,
I test out his throne. I repurpose his sacrificial altar as the seat of
Jen, both judge and jury, sending my husband summons and edicts,
blessings or punishment. I want Jared to get what he deserves—
pleasure or pain, peace or turmoil—in response to his actions. I
proclaim my own excellencies and self-adoring kudos, instead of
those of the one who continues to call me out of darkness and
into his light.[3]

I forget the order of my High Priest. Jesus lives as the go-
between—praying for us and advocating on our behalf.[4]

> Since we have a great priest over the house of God, let us
> draw near with a true heart in full assurance of faith . . .
> And let us consider how to stir up one another to love
> and good works, not neglecting to meet together, as is
> the habit of some, but encouraging one another . . .
> (Heb. 10:21–22, 24–25)

Of all the things I provoke, love doesn't jump to the top of the
list. I incite frustration. Instigate activity. Sometimes irritate to
compliance. So how is a woman to stir up love? I wanted to come
to you with a list of fifty things, proclaiming, "This is how . . ." to
stir and meet and encourage all the goodness. Fortunately, God
rerouted me.

Stir Up Love

The purpose of these pages isn't to offer a catalog of *hows*. Marriage isn't one-size-fits-all. The blueprint for building a safe haven in our relationships relies on Christ as the cornerstone. In him, we are built together into a dwelling place.[5]

The body of Christ fashioned as the church.

Wives joined with our husbands.

> Let us think of ways to motivate one another to acts of
> love and good works. (Heb. 10:24 NLT)

Reflect upon your beloved. Where is he in this season of life, in his career, ministry, and walk of faith? Contemplate what he enjoys, where he falters, and who God created him to be. These observations will lead you to the practical *hows* of stirring love and building safety in your relationship.

It's also worth noting what impedes this love, tainting it with sour undertones. Nothing contaminates the sweet aroma of consideration like the pungent odor of unforgiveness.

Once upon a time—in Jen's storybook—a king meets with his accountant and finds a large number of unsettled debts. Being a prudent leader, he settles accounts with his servants, instead of carrying such a heavy load of unpaid bills. So he calls for Lucy.

She comes to meet with the king, her note worth more than she could hope to earn in her lifetime.[6]

Lucy falls to her knees, pleading for patience.

In compassion, the king does her one better. He forgives her debt.

Moved by his generosity, the young maiden leaves the palace, clapping and dancing. She buys flowers for the table and ingredients for a feast. Her debt is no more! But when Lucy arrives at her sweet cottage, her joy dissipates. Her husband was supposed to take out the garbage this morning, yet there it sits, a rotting fish smell stinking up the kitchen. She puts the blossoms in a jar, recalling how nice it would be for her man to buy her flowers, like Susan's guy did for his bride. And what about the role of leader—when was he going to learn to do that?

By the time Lucy's mate arrives home, she's moved him from the bedroom to the couch and then sentenced him to the doghouse.

"Pay back what you owe me."

"Honey, have patience with me. I'm working on it."

In the record of this parable in Matthew 18, the servant throws his debtor into prison. The master hears of this wickedness and decides not to cancel the debt after all.

"So also my heavenly Father will do to every one of you,
    if you do not forgive your brother from your heart."
    (Matt. 18:35)

As we stir up love, we must not fold in unforgiveness. This bitter root contaminates our spousal interactions, prompting us to keep records of our husbands' wrongs. If God did such a thing, we could never stand before him.[7] We ask the Lord for his provision, to accomplish his will, deliver us from the enemy, and forgive our debts *as we forgive* our debtors.[8]

I've found that a hesitation to forgive is often coupled with a delay in repentance. We don't feel safe enough to say, "I'm sorry" first, seeing an admission of guilt as too high a price to pay for emotional intimacy. When I send my pardons with attached strings and harbored feelings of injustice, I forget that what I give will be given back to me, coming in "good measure, pressed down, shaken together, running over, poured into [my] lap." The measuring cup I use is refilled and returned.[9] So I drag my feet when it comes time to repent, assuming my mate will misuse this new upper hand, instead of forgiving freely.

. . . forgive as quickly and completely as the Master forgave you. (Col. 3:13 *The Message*)

I want my hubby to cherish me like Christ loves the church and to fill the role of spiritual leader in our home. But there's not a marriage academy to graduate from before our men pop the important diamond-studded question. In the same way we learn this wife thing as we go, our spouses do the same, many of them without godly examples of leadership to refer to in their own families. They survive the dating, proposal, wedding, honeymoon stages, and now come face to face with the giant mountain that is marriage. We grab their hands and affirm their role, "Take it away, Spiritual Leader!" Half of us have no clue what that means; we're just grateful it's the guys' job to figure that out.

I imagine it like Eve's first labor and delivery. Adam knew his wife in the biblical *knowing* and she conceived. He could tell things were different, what with her cravings, mood swings, and bulging belly. As months passed, they realized Eve carried a stranger in her body that would need to come out—without Lamaze classes or *What to Expect* books. The only recorded insight this first couple had into the miracle of childbirth came in one simple sentence God spoke to Eve, before he sent them out of the Garden of Eden:

"I will surely multiply your pain in childbearing; in pain you shall bring forth children." (Gen. 3:16)

Oh, the pressure on poor Adam to figure things out. To calm his wife's concerns. No midwife to boil water or catch the baby. Eve needing her man to be there for her, and he without knowledge of what to do. I wonder how long they deliberated on cutting the umbilical cord, and if Eve broke all the bones in his hand while pushing and contracting, contracting and pushing.

Cain came into the world "with the help of the Lord,"[10] as did their future children. I bring this same hope to our marriages.

> Your husband will lead with the help of the Lord.

Just as we need time to develop healthy wifestyle habits, our men need grace and forgiveness to become the spouses we yearn for. Your wedding day blessed your man with the mantle of spousal leadership. Now he must learn how to carry it.

Draw Near

. . . let us draw near with a true heart . . . (Heb. 10:22)

Yes, it's rewarding when everything clicks into place, when your mate knows what you prefer and moves ahead to accommodate. But in the spectrum of *Great* (he knows me so well) and *Horrible* (he doesn't notice at all), sometimes we are wise to accept what's in between: *Good* (I share and he considers me).

Dear friend, tell your man what you're looking for and why it means so much to you. We must take the time to figure out what we really want and communicate it to our spouses instead of expecting them to somehow just . . . *know.*

Some of us hesitate to reveal the true desires of our hearts, because once we're exposed, we risk rejection. If I tell Jared that holding hands in public makes me feel like he's showing his love to the world and wants to be associated with me as his wife, then I risk feeling abandoned if he doesn't reach for my fingertips. It's safer to be angry than vulnerable, so I wait for months, maybe years, hoping he'll maneuver the labyrinth of my heart on his own. Making quips along the way—"Trey just grabbed Kelsey's hand; that's so sweet"—I blame him for not catching the hint. Neither of us realizes it, but I'm chipping away at the covering of our safe haven, feeling deserted because I withhold myself from my spouse instead of drawing near.

Come to your hubby with a true heart. Don't tarnish the integrity of your word with hidden opinions or intentions. Let your yes be yes.[11] If you have thoughts on a matter, as is often good and right, share them. The same must be encouraged of our men, no matter how different their viewpoint is from our own.

Communicate what you hope for—not to demand, but to *commune* with him. Build upon the intimacy of your connection, exchanging thoughts and feelings on a deeper level.

The concept of spiritual leadership is of particular importance as we draw near to our husbands. Scripture instructs our men to love with sacrifice and consideration. They are to bring up their children in the training and instruction of the Lord[12] and to live as examples of Christ. But sometimes we develop our own checklists of what this is to look like:

- Leading family devotionals
- Praying before meals at large gatherings
- Public commendations, preaching, or teaching
- Sharing Scripture at dinner

While nothing is wrong with these activities, they are preferences, not requirements for leadership. We crowd around with wife-imposed expectations, assuming they'll learn to swim if we throw them out into open waters, calling on quiet husbands to give public toasts and newfound believers to come to Jesus today and lead Bible studies tomorrow.

Talk with your husband if those demonstrations of faith are important to you and see if he agrees to assume those activities. If not, let them go. Ask God to give your man the inner *character* of a leader—a quality of heart that comes out in every conversation and interaction, not just in particular religious activities or personality traits.

Full Assurance of Faith

> . . . in full assurance of faith . . . (Heb. 10:22)

Safety in our marriages means making it OK to try and fail. To say, "I think we can find a better idea" without causing injury. When one spouse falls down, the other is there to dust them off and help them up again.[13]

Trial and error produced some of the most cherished experiences in my marriage, including but not limited to our rocky start with date nights. I like a good plan, and Jared excelled at spontaneity. Our first few spur-of-the-moment dinner-and-a-movie date nights were fine. But when my birthday rolled around about three months into our relationship, I realized some things had to be said.

I had a business trip that week and took extraordinary measures to make it back midafternoon on the day of my birthday, promising my evening to Jared for whatever he had planned.

The whole flight home, I daydreamed of romantic preparations. Flowers and chocolate. Reservations or surprise parties.

Jared picked me up at the airport and started driving us back to his house. "I thought we'd take it easy tonight. Maybe order a pizza and watch a movie."

"But—today is my birthday." My voice cracked as I blinked back tears.

"Oh, I figured you'd be tired after a busy week. I wanted to give you time to relax and recover."

I thought this guy liked me, and here he was, already not reading my mind. I wish I could say we handled the conversation well. That my emotions stayed in check and Jared planned incredible dates from that night forward. All things went sour before they became sweet again, but I'll spare you those tart details.

What I *will* say is that my husband now plans fantastic date nights, with themes and clues and adventures.

BONUS: Download the helpful article "The Importance of Dating after 'I Do'" at thejenweaver.com/wifestylebonus

Even better than our dating escapades, though, is the way we've learned to talk through our failures—building on them as foundations for future successes. Here's how we ATTACK the situation, and I hope some of these steps will help you as well:

Acknowledge how things have been up until this point. This includes recognizing the role I played in creating the situation I don't like.

"I'm upset because I thought you would plan something special for my birthday. That type of consideration speaks love to me, and I realize now I could have shared my expectations upfront."

Tell him what you'd like and why.

"In the future, I'd enjoy it if you planned our dates in advance. Making arrangements for unique activities tells me you value our time together and want it to be special."

Talk about alternate approaches.

Here's where we get creative. Jared and I have planned date nights together and have alternated weeks planning outings the other person would enjoy. We've brainstormed date ideas and kept a running list to choose from. And from time to time, one of us will just come flat out and request an activity—including take-out and a movie night in.

Ask if that's something he wants and how you can help.

The difference between *offering* and *demanding* comes in the asking. Just because I suggest a change doesn't mean Jared needs to make it. Alternate approaches are suggestions, and we are both free to continue the conversation if our expectations aren't matching up.

Commend his successes.

Even with hurt feelings and disappointment, the evening wasn't doomed for failure. Jared considered me in keeping our date low-key; he just didn't have a correct understanding of what I wanted. He picked me up on time and made himself available for the whole afternoon and evening, knowing I had done the same. After working through tears and talking through better plans for the future, we moved on and had fun. We ate, played games, and cuddled on the couch watching a sweet chick flick. If I kept my focus on the failures, I would have missed the twinkling stars of his success, hurting more than just our time together that evening.

Kiss and move on.

Don't belabor the issue. What's done is done and everyone can do better next time.

BONUS: Download an ATTACK travel card at
thejenweaver.com/wifestylebonus

Before we transition from this topic of safe havens leaving room for mistakes, it's worth noting that sometimes our ATTACK model comes with a bonus "A": Anger.

As a friend once told me, "Anger is a root. Not a fruit. It's evidence of something deeper." As you **acknowledge** how things have been, go ahead and acknowledge your feelings on the subject. There's nothing wrong with the emotion of anger; the issue arises with how we handle it.

Be angry and do not sin; do not let the sun go down on your
anger, and give no opportunity to the devil. (Eph. 4:26–27)

Once upon a time, I'd argue my perspective into the wee hours of
the night, preventing the sun from setting on my anger but ignoring
the other parts of this verse—"give no opportunity to the devil."
With heated words and hot tears, I forged close bonds between my
anger and sin, closing one door to the enemy while opening gates,
windows, and air vents. I could be "right" in my facts but wrong in
how I handled the situation. The Bible doesn't say, "don't let the sun
go down until you solve the problem." Acknowledge the issue and
address your emotion in ways that contribute to the resolution. You
may find that in that moment, it's best to choose not to be angry.
Don't buy the lie—*you* control your emotions. Release them for
the moment and return to work through the conflict when you
can respond better.

Stop being angry! Turn from your rage! Do not lose
your temper—it only leads to harm. (Ps. 37:8 NLT)

Meet Together with Encouragement

. . . not neglecting to meet together, as is the habit of
some, but encouraging one another . . . (Heb. 10:25)

Meet together. I'm not talking date nights, bible studies, or physical
intimacy—although all those things are often included. Find safety
in each other's presence, not just when glancing up from to-do lists
or hurried meals. Make time that is void of working and doing and
striving. Just *be* together.

Sometimes even absent of talking, Jared and I sit together in
silence. I pull myself out of the steady hum of whirling brain cogs
and ticking timelines. Putting away my phone, I think about this

man in the seat next to me. The feeling of his fingers interlaced with mine. Noticing the age lines that have developed since we first met. Remembering the moves and tears and goofy kitchen dance parties. The battles we've fought and won. For all I know, he's sitting there thinking about nothing at all, as men are able to do. But when he glances in my direction, God's grace fills the moment and we *see* one another. We meet together.

> Creating safe havens in our homes means bringing our dirt out into the light.

I savor these moments together, but over the years, I've also had to learn to be OK when things get uncomfortable. I'm a natural peace*keeper*, not a peace*maker*. In the past, conflict made me break out in hives, and I'd hide hurt feelings and offenses under relationship rugs with the best of them. Pretending that nothing was wrong made every problem more painful. Creating safe havens in our homes means bringing our dirt out into the light. Not to point fingers or cast blame, but to clean the soot out of the house.

Even in the most difficult conversations, I want my words to contribute grace and mercy to those that hear them, speaking life to my husband, and to my own heart.[14] Mercy withholds the bad that is deserved. Grace goes a step further and gives unmerited good.

In our zeal to receive the benefits of spiritual leadership, I've found some common mistakes: ***Men are often gun-shy and women are particular.***

Gun-shy guys are all or nothing. They put off and resist leadership roles because it scares the pants off them. Intimidated by such a large, unfamiliar role, many men go from one extreme to the other. They jump into this leadership thing, and they commit *hard*. Suddenly, they feel the pressure to make every decision. To come up with all the thoughts and plans on their own, assuming that being the *leader* means they must do all the deciding solo—Big Chief Decision Maker. Heavy is the noggin that wears that head-dress, because the head is still part of the body; it doesn't wander off and do things alone.[15] Being in charge means stewarding resources, receiving counsel, and taking care of the people you lead.

On the female side of the equation, we tend to be particular. We want to pick and choose what it means for our men to lead, how it looks, and when (or if) we have to listen to them. I'm all for Jared leading when it means sacrifice and consideration.

Spiritual covering to take responsibility for the hard choices? Yes and amen.

But I don't like it so much when he's bringing the Word to instruct or correct an area of my life. He addresses a character flaw, and I'm quick to throw one back at him, rebuffing his insight because I can, even if he's right.

Now we could sit here and draw lines in the sand, committing to turn our homes, our relationships, and our presence as wives into safe havens . . . as soon as our husbands do. We could wait and dawdle, blaming areas of insecurity on their inaptitude.

Or we could make the change ourselves, throw out those huge deceptive rugs we've swept everything under, and work on building peace. And maybe as we build their confidence, attributing courage in the grace of our safe haven, they'll change as a by-product.

> Enjoy him as a blessing from God, and that is what he will become.

Acknowledge the good your husband does. The way he cares, serves, provides, and loves. Make allowance—not excuses—for his faults and forgive offenses.[16] Surround your husband with a sense of courage through your interactions. Offer him a seat *in courage*, smack dab in the middle of fearlessness. Let him build the nerve to lead and love in valor because he knows you have his back. You won't reject him if he falters, or rub his nose in his shortcomings. Enjoy him as a blessing from God, and that is what he will become.

BONUS: Man-to-man encouragement from my husband to yours at thejenweaver.com/wifestylebonus

Wifestyle: Guarded or Grace

The guarded wife is risk adverse. She avoids vulnerability and conflict by letting issues build up inside until they explode. She wants her husband to be the "spiritual leader" but often fights his attempts because she doesn't understand what this means. She hesitates to share her wants and needs out of fear of being rejected, and often feels discouraged and abandoned when these same desires aren't met.

The grace wifestyle is marked by compassion and encouragement. She recognizes her husband is learning how to be a leader just as she is learning to follow his lead, and she makes intentional choices to bring peace and grace into their interactions. This wife experiences a greater level of partnership with her husband as they have freedom to be their true selves, absent of judgment and full of forgiveness as they grow into God's callings on their lives.

Is Your Wifestyle Guarded or Grace-Filled?

Take the themes of this chapter to a whole new level of practical application. Circle the responses that best represent your answer to each question.

	A	B
I hate being the one to apologize first.	True	False
True love is my man knowing what I want or need without me telling him.	True	False
I've defined "spiritual leadership" as external activities like leading devotionals or praying out loud.	True	False
I often feel like my husband avoids having difficult conversations with me.	True	False
Past hurts keep my hubby and I from opening up to each other.	True	False
Please circle words in each column that best describe your recent attitudes or behaviors toward your husband. Circle all that apply.	Reserved Begrudging Indifferent	Vulnerable Forgiving Teachable

Please tally your results. "A" answers exhibit a guarded wifestyle. "B" answers show a grace-filled wifestyle.

Ways to Develop a Grace-Filled Wifestyle

Don't settle for a guarded relationship with your husband. Use these steps to approach your marriage with grace and contribute to building a safe haven in your heart and home.

- Build a vocabulary of grace-filled words. Approach your husband with gentle feedback and questions not accusations.
  - "I have some ideas to help us with . . ."
  - "Can I share a few concerns I have . . . ?"
  - "Would you like my assistance in . . . ?"
- Reflect on what you know of your husband—who he is, his strengths, weaknesses, insecurities, and preferences. List ways you can show considerate love based on the intimate details you know about his life.

- Take a few minutes at the end of each day to observe how God has blessed you. Perhaps this time occurs during supper or right before you go to bed. Tell your man about these sweet demonstrations of God's love, strengthening your spousal connection through shared gratitude.
- Trust doesn't grow in the wild; it's nurtured through intentional choices and consideration. Prove trustworthy with your husband's heart, dreams, goals, and concerns. Make your marriage a safe haven by contributing trust in honest responses and sharing your heart through humble communication.
- Pay attention to how you respond to your hubby's attempts to lead, teach, and serve. If your reactions seem to discourage him from trying again, consider ways to change your approach in thought, word, tone, attitude, and action.

What Do You Think?

- Do you include relational threats in your marriage vocabulary? Do you allow embittered friends to encourage you to choose a similar path?
- Have you let circumstances weaken the safety of your marriage relationship? What choices can you make today to strengthen your connection?
- Are you slow to forgive your husband?
- What heart desires are you withholding from your spouse, hoping he'll somehow figure them out on his own?
- Have you defined "spiritual leadership" through specific religious activities instead of godly character?

Real Life #Wifestylin: Danielle's Story

It was two weeks before Christmas. I was eight months pregnant and preparing our two-year-old daughter for her soon-to-be life with a sibling. I trusted my husband with all my heart and loved him deeply. Life was good.

Winding down for the night, something told me to look at Brian's phone, sitting on the kitchen counter. Minutes later I stood in front of our house, throwing his cell phone on the pavement as hard as I could. I marched to the garage and used a shovel to smash the disgusting images on its screen. I was too outraged to pray, and with our daughter on my hip, I began packing up the last five years. Many of you can understand my feelings of abandonment, shock, and emptiness. I never wanted to see my husband again. Ever.

I was so afraid. But God didn't abandon me. Somehow I knew everything was going to be OK. You have to understand, that way of thinking is not like me. I was more of a "dump him and move on" kind of girl. But God had other plans.

That hard night now happened over four years ago. Brian and I are still working on our relationship, and maintaining trust is a constant process. But I'll tell you that God showed up that day, and he never left. He has restored our marriage and continually renews my confidence in his faithfulness. Despite our ups and downs, we are closer now than we have ever been—both in marriage and in our relationships with Jesus.

–Danielle, married in 2007

Brian's betrayal threatened the safe haven of his marriage in ways no woman should ever have to face. But in that moment, with all the pain and tears, Danielle didn't leave. She chose forgiveness and reconciliation, and through her actions began the process of rebuilding trust in her marriage. And this couple continues to repeat those choices, over and over again, as God continues his work in restoring health to their relationship.

CHAPTER TEN

The *Blessing* of Intimacy

"And in that day the mountains shall drip sweet wine . . ."

Joel 3:18

We all have our own wedding memories. Special days that come equipped with horror stories of misplaced groomsmen, wilted flowers, drunk uncles, or lost honeymoon luggage. For now, imagine the following story as your own.

The joy-filled wedding fades into the fog of yesterday, as you and your beloved embark on day two of your honeymoon, a tropical cruise. After a long day of travel, sun-tanned fun on the lido deck, and a huge dinner in the ship's dining room, you retire to your quarters—him to lounge in wait and you to primp in the closet-sized bathroom.

Being only the second night of your marriage, you take extra time getting ready, building his anticipation. You shower to remove any hint of the morning's airport smell. Your new silk teddy rests just right. Hair styled and eyelids smoked to seductive perfection, you fold back the accordion door to your tiny suite with sultry allure to find your lover—asleep. He doesn't even stir when your heavy discouragement plops down on the bed. If you're anything like me, that's when the waterworks start.

If he is this disinterested on the second night of our honeymoon, what chance does that leave for the rest of our marriage?

As someone who "imagines" such a nightmare with precise accuracy, I come with hope! God offers a plan to deepen every expression of spousal intimacy. Establishing deep connections with our husbands goes far beyond the *act* of marriage.

- **Emotional closeness**: Entrusting deep feelings and secret dreams
- **Intellectual attachment**: Goal setting and partnership
- **Spiritual oneness**: When we pray, worship, give thanks, and study Scripture together—allowing us small glimpses into our mates' relationships with Jesus
- **Physical connection**: Where lovemaking melds two hearts into one

Every other section of this book is about building emotional, intellectual, and spiritual intimacy. But for these few pages, we must give due attention to the taboo topic of . . . sex.

> If you've been sexually assaulted, abused, or mistreated, please prayerfully consider if now is the best time for you to read this chapter. Discussing sexual intimacy can trigger painful emotions and memories for survivors, and if these topics are not helpful for you to address in this season, please move on to the next chapter without reading.

I feel the strong need to pray for God's protection before we continue. The enemy wars against our marriages, and one of his favorite battlefields is the arena of physical intimacy. If we are not careful as we reveal lies and pitfalls, we can see a burden plaguing another woman and pick it up as a new weight on our own marriages.

Please pray with me.

Dear God, Thank you for the way you desire to bless my marriage with deep intimacy. Please guard my heart and mind from any attack of the enemy. As I read about possible insecurities and the blessings you want to bring, provide your unmistakable direction. If I struggle with an area, speak to it clearly and plainly in my heart. If the topic does not apply, help me move on without picking it up. I refuse to receive bondage through these pages, only freedom. In Jesus's name, Amen.

Sex in the Past
No one comes to marriage with a sexual blank slate.

My *fictional* friend Morgan came into marriage with her virginity intact. Proud to have saved herself for her husband and impassioned by pent up affection, she carried high expectations with her virgin card. *She waited all this time. God should bless her with an incredible sex life, right?* But Morgan felt embarrassed by her lack of knowledge of what to do when, how best to please him, what would feel good to her, and where in God's name should she put her hands? Her husband seemed satisfied, but he didn't match the Hollywood depictions of never-satiated sex drives and nightly marathons of bedsheet wrestling. *Was he even interested? Did he still find her beautiful?* Even while wanting her man to desire her, Morgan struggled to accept her own sex drive as inherently good, instead of a temptation to overcome. To make matters worse, years of antisex conditioning left her hypermodest, and she felt embarrassed that her body didn't tout lingerie model perfection.

Tiffany, Morgan's BFF in this fabricated world, also found problems in her intimate married life—but due to a different background. Tiffany's sex life started before she met Travis, and continued during their dating relationship. Somewhat embarrassed by her past, she struggled with comparing her husband to old partners. Their shared escapades once carried an air of danger, but the thrill of misbehavior disappeared in the purity of a marriage bed, contributing to her diminished satisfaction. Her husband couldn't seem to get enough, and he often requested activities or positions she didn't feel comfortable with now that they were married. Tiffany knew Travis had an active sexual history, and she wondered if he also compared her performance to past events. *Did he imagine being with someone else?*

A virgin on my wedding night, I can relate to aspects of both these stories. I came into marriage with preconceived ideas, unrealistic expectations, emotional baggage, and some unfortunate unchosen experiences as a child. Whether your sexual history presents you to your husband as chaste or experienced, now is a good a time to start unpacking some of the sexual baggage every couple wishes they lost on their way to the altar.

Talk about it. Sin festers and multiplies in darkness. Everything good grows in the light. Unless you're commending his actions, don't try talking about aspects of sexual performance in the exact moment of intimacy, or during the delicious afterglow. Discuss everything with your spouse, and I mean *everything*, in a time, place, and manner that edifies your relationship.

BONUS: Access a list of additional resources for sexual healing at thejenweaver.com/wifestylebonus

Sexy Present

Sex is not a worldly passion. Lust is. The enemy can't create; he only counterfeits. He touts the cheap knockoff of extramarital intercourse as the real deal, when it can't compare to the gift of intimacy God created in a sacred committed relationship. The Lord dedicated an entire book to recount how Solomon and his bride delighted in each other. And Solomon's chick was *into* him, even though he compared her to a horse, her hair to a flock of goats, her nose to a tower, and her abs to a heap of wheat.[1] Those are fighting words in my house, but it seemed to work for his Beloved.

> Sex is not a worldly passion.

So here's my question. Has the enemy stolen the blessing of intimacy in your marriage? I'm not talking about what happened before—hopefully you're working through that—but in this present moment, right here and now, would you describe your marriage as sexy, or have you turned your heart away?

In the book of Joel, a prophet by the same name delivers a warning to the Israelite people.

> "A black day! A Doomsday! Clouds with no silver lining!
> Like dawn light moving over the mountains, a huge
> army is coming. . . . Wildfire burns everything before
> this army and fire licks up everything in its wake. Before
> it arrives, the country is like the Garden of Eden. When
> it leaves, it is Death Valley. Nothing escapes unscathed.
> The locust army seems all horses—galloping horses,
> an army of horses. . . . They arrive like an earthquake,

sweep through like a tornado. Sun and moon turn out
their lights, stars black out. . . . But there's also this, it's
not too late—God's personal Message!—'Come back
to me and really mean it!' . . . Change your life, not just
your clothes . . ." (Joel 2:2–4, 10, 12–13 *The Message*)

Our God is always ready to cancel catastrophe, but we must
change our hearts, not just our outward appearance.[2] Investing in
the physical intimacy of your marriage means more than tolerating
your husband's requests, initiating sex, or wearing lingerie.

We must turn our hearts toward our husbands to receive God's
blessing of intimacy.

Where you've turned away in the past because he's hurt you or
harped on an insecurity, return with your heart.

Where you've felt used or unappreciated, turn.

If you've found other forms of release and emotional fulfillment, reinstall your affection.

Do you compare your mate to another man, wishing he was
more like your friend's husband or the spouse you imagine in your
head? Don't covet what belongs to your neighbor.[3] Asking God for
the good desires he placed in our hearts is different from creating
comparison charts between our husband and another's. Realign
your heart's perspective.

God created men as visual beings. They appreciate curves, lines,
and visible stimuli. But for most women, our connection is mental
and emotional. Our attire stimulates them even if our thoughts and
emotions are focused elsewhere. We can talk without really communicating, conversing without intimacy. We must turn our hearts.

> Don't let the enemy tarnish the gift God offers
> for your marriage.

Not sure how to approach conversations about your sex life? Here are some helpful questions to begin this dialogue with your spouse:

Impurities

- Do past experiences pollute your marital enjoyment?
- Has pornography tarnished the purity of your marital intimacy?
- Do the enemy's lies repeat in your mind–poking at insecurities about your body, your connection, what he wants or needs, or your mutual satisfaction, and replace the anticipation of fun with obligatory dread?

Expectations

- Do you expect God to bless your sex life?
- Regardless of your experiences until this point, do you believe that God wants you to receive pleasure from your mate?
- Do you carry unspoken expectations for how your spouse will romance you?

Insecurities

- Are you confident during sexual intimacy or self-conscious?
- Do you let your hubby appreciate and enjoy your body, even features you may not like?
- Do your words and actions contribute to your husband's insecurities or help alleviate them?

Injuries

- Do you find your marriage bed a place of safety and fun, or of emotional injury and guilt?

- Has your man betrayed your trust in the past, making it difficult for you to openly express and give of yourself now?
- Do either or both of you carry emotional or sexual injuries from past relationships? These may include unwanted encounters such as rape or molestation, and if so, I encourage you to seek therapy to work through these issues. You cannot find sexual health together if one of you carries untreated trauma from the past. Years into my marriage, I realized that while I had forgiven Jared for having sex with other women before coming to Christ, I hadn't allowed God to bring healing to that area of our union. I wanted to ignore it rather than address it, and the enemy used Jared's past to inflict new injuries on our present marriage.

Enjoyment

- What things do you especially enjoy during lovemaking with your mate? Does he know you enjoy them?
- Are there secret desires you haven't spoken of, out of fear of rejection?

Pay close attention to any areas that are difficult for you to discuss with your spouse. Anything you *withhold* from your mate indicates a *foothold* (the enemy's temporary position as he gains ground) or enemy *stronghold* (an established fortress). Hiding only harms your relationship, and opening yourself up to this dialogue opens your marriage to the blessing of intimacy.

I wouldn't dare tell you what intimacy should look like for your marriage. These norms vary based on the values of your community and the way your family operates. You must determine with your husband how sexual intimacy is expressed in your relationship, ensuring that each partner feels loved, respected, and considered. If any encounter leaves you feeling less than treasured, talk with your mate. Involve a counselor or Christian sex therapist as needed. Don't let the enemy tarnish the gift God offers for your marriage, whether through misuse or neglect—these corrosive properties are wielded by men and women alike.

The M Words

The sexual mistreatment of wives sickens me, especially when it happens within Christian marriages. We've talked about how abuse is never acceptable and how godly submission doesn't lead to sin, but please humor me as I reiterate it here. Scripture instructs us to submit to our husbands "as is fitting in the Lord."[4] Suitable responses under the headship of Christ *cannot* include actions inconsistent with his character. Domineering men may take 1 Corinthians out of context to demand sex from their wives.

> The husband should give to his wife her conjugal rights, and likewise the wife to her husband. For the wife does not have authority over her own body, but the husband does. Likewise the husband does not have authority over his own body, but the wife does. (1 Cor. 7:3–4)

If a husband has authority over his wife's body to command sex, then a wife has authority over his body to dictate that he not receive what he requests, and the sad sexless cycle continues. Thankfully, most of our men are not horrid dictators, though we pray for women in such dire circumstances.

As we move through these pages, we must next recognize that the sexual mistreatment of husbands is also problematic. While less common for a wife to physically overpower her husband, wives can mishandle sexual connections in other ways.

Modesty. Women are to dress "modestly, with decency and propriety."[5] But consider what appropriate attire means when you are alone with your husband. Lace? Sequins? Silk? Unless both of you agree that sex is best wearing bed sheets with conveniently placed holes, proper attire in front of your husband is . . . naked.

> Modesty is virtue. Insecurity breeds isolation.

I'm not advocating that we structure our homes like nudist colonies—although if you're in that yummy prechildren season, *consider the perks*. Some of us block our husbands out of our lives by calling *insecurities* another name. Modesty is virtue. Insecurity breeds isolation. Are there areas of your daily life that you withhold from your husband under the guise of propriety? If he can't see you naked unless you're "being intimate," you're limiting the physical intimacy of your relationship to sex. It's not sinful for your husband to admire your assets in uplifting and honorable ways as you dress for work in the morning. To see you in the shower, or to walk in on you in the bathroom—although there may be other reasons to avoid that. *You*, all of your curves and rounded parts, are fully appropriate for your hubby's enjoyment. To live otherwise tells your spouse that his desires for you are inappropriate, unwelcome, and sinful. In reality, your beautiful form is part of God's marital blessing of intimacy.

The Bible instructs married couples not to withhold from one another unless it comes from mutual agreement for a limited time.[12] This is a great standard for all aspects of our sex lives. Does the activity align with purity according to God and match up with mutual agreement? Free from pressure or threats, is it something you both want to try? Does it pass the Spirit's conviction for keeping your marriage bed pure?[13] Then please partake, you lucky woman. Let that wedding band on your finger free you from your garter belt.

Before moving on, I want to speak to a related issue of sexual propriety and thank Dr. Juli Slattery for sharing her thoughts and Dr. Jody Dillow's research in her book *25 Questions You're Afraid to Ask about Love, Sex, and Intimacy*.[6] Since many aspects of physical enjoyment are corrupted by the enemy, it can be hard to find the boundary lines for purity. Scripture limits sexual expression to the following:

- Between a husband and wife[7]
- No
  - ♦ extramarital participants[8]
  - ♦ homosexual partners[9]
  - ♦ animals or incest
- Sex isn't limited to intercourse, or even sexual actions that stop before "going all the way." Sexual purity involves our eyes, mind, and heart, thus including pornography and explicit romance novels as aspects of sexual sin.

"You have heard that it was said, 'You shall not commit adultery.' But I say to you that everyone who looks at a woman with lustful intent has already committed adultery with her in his heart." (Matt. 5:27-28–emphasis mine)

While BDSM (bondage, dominance, sadism, and masochism) isn't specifically addressed in Scripture, these demeaning acts oppose God's character and the way he instructs us to care for our spouses with respect and love–men cherishing their wives with tender consideration,[10] ensuring physical intimacy honors their bride so the groom's prayers are not hindered.[11]

Manipulation. *Virginity* is my gift for my husband. But *sex* is a gift God gives to *both* of us. To treat physical intimacy as something I can give, take away, or barter for household chores, romantic outings, or ideal foreplay is a perversion of God's generosity, like signing my name as gift-giver for a present another guest brought to the wedding. Jared and I belong to each other, and God-blessed abstinence comes from *mutual* agreement.[14]

> *Virginity* is my gift for my husband. But *sex* is a gift God gives to *both* of us.

Sexual manipulation often comes back to the desire to control. Our husbands may not respond to conversations or shouting matches, but if we withhold sex, we coerce temporary compliance. We also sacrifice our chances at emotional intimacy because we use our husbands' vulnerability against them. As wives, we must be willing to risk rejection for the sake of intimacy. We must give up control—not to become a pushover but to become a partner.

Lover Not Mother

I left off one final "M" word from the previous section:

Mothering. Recall a time when you were enthralled with your husband—maybe yesterday, your last anniversary, or during your honeymoon. Passion and desire heightened, holding you captive in the moment. A physical encounter, a romantic evening, or a passing glance spiked your heart rate. Go back to how you felt, imagine the surroundings, and recall your spicy thoughts. All right, which one of those memories relate to motherhood?

Marital passion doesn't leave any room for mothering tendencies. A wife cannot melt, captivated by male prowess, and wonder if he ate vegetables at lunch.

God designed your marriage relationship for intense love. A holy designation.

As a wife, it's your right to be a lover. So why default to mothering?

Mother knows best is a household phrase for a reason—when it comes to her children, she often does. But carrying this perspective into your marriage emasculates your husband and hinders his ability to satisfy you sexually.

If you are a mother of children, I commend you for your hard work at a job that never ends and a vocation that never gets a vacation. Motherhood is a noble calling, and we approach our roles with deliberate intention as we take prenatal vitamins, research schools, and plan carpools. Yet sometimes mothering abilities sneak into our spousal relationships in a less obvious manner—even for those without real life children to blame it on.

Noble intent paired with poor execution leads to a lot of unfortunate mothering episodes, especially for newlywed Jen Weaver. This current Jen, version 7.0, has made some significant upgrades, so we can learn from the mistakes of previous editions.

New hubby Jared admitted to a faulty memory, so I self-appointed myself as his live 4D Outlook calendar, especially for super important trivial things like taking daily multivitamins. We'd sit at the dining room table—a.k.a. coffee table in front of the TV, because in the BC (before children) years, meals meant binge watching—and I'd casually glance over at his setup. Food. Beverage. Utensils. No vitamin. About halfway through the meal, the original Mrs. Weaver would make a casual offer.

"I'm going to the kitchen to grab [some unnecessary condiment]. Would you like me to get your vitamin?"

So sly. Other times, the offer came with greater force.

"Make sure to take your vitamin."

Or the always appreciated random benefit statement: "Vitamins are best taken with food."

A few months into the marriage, my vitamin-stuffed husband confronted the issue with a gentle question. "Do you think you're my mom?"

Shock betrayed my face. *Of course not. I'm your helpful, doting wife, who's just looking out for you.*

He asked me to knock it off. I tried to support him in ways he hadn't asked for and never wanted. I claimed the title of Vitamin Enforcer all on my own—a role he found annoying and emasculating, as if he were a child whose mommy still took care of him.

With the upgrade of my wifely operating system, I asked my husband if he *wanted* a reminder for his vitamins. (I know, novel idea right?) He agreed to an *occasional* assist, and I watched my word choice when providing reminders, to communicate as a helpmate rather than his mom.

BONUS: Download the helpful article
"Top Ten Helpful Phrases as a Helpmate" at
thejenweaver.com/wifestylebonus

Since the maternal instinct comes innately to many of us, it's easy to fall into the trap of mothering your husband. Perhaps it's urging him to wear a coat in winter's Icelandic blizzard or discouraging a second plate of fried chicken with scary mom eyes. Maybe it's the constant nagging to change his priorities to match yours or the innate desire to make decisions for him, discounting his perspectives as those of a less-informed minor in need of guidance. If you view yourself in a caretaker's role, you'll act in the same manner. Continue to respond as a mom, and your husband may perceive you this way. Talk about an easy way to erode sexual intimacy.

A mothering wife forces compliance, rather than forging a life together as a partner. Becoming the mother in the small aspects of your man's life means you cannot expect him to lead in the big aspects of yours. Times of difficulty are when we recognize the need for authority the most. Will you find your mate strong for the task, or is he wiping boogers on your apron because that's the pattern you both created for your lives?

> Becoming the mother in the small aspects of your man's life means you cannot expect him to lead in the big aspects of yours.

Spousal guardianship may indicate that you're trying to fulfill other needs. Is this a way to maintain control? Are you building a sense of self-worth by how your husband depends on you? Did you pick your man knowing he'd bend to your will? If these questions describe you, change how you relate to your mate. Assuming a spousal parental role keeps wives in a mommy box, unable to break free and experience other aspects of intimacy and fulfillment as women. And let's be real—you're nowhere near old enough to be his mother.

Redeem

We like to believe that we can disregard the past—that anything bad, nasty, or distasteful about yesterday doesn't matter today. We try to hide these mistakes in trunks locked like nesting dolls before burying them at the bottom of don't-talk-about-it ocean.

As Morgan and Tiffany found out earlier in the chapter, God offers a better option.

Let him redeem it.

"And in that day the mountains shall drip sweet wine,
and the hills shall flow with milk, and all the streambeds
of Judah shall flow with water; and a fountain shall

come forth from the house of the LORD and water the Valley . . ." (Joel 3:18)

We've spent this chapter discussing physical intimacy because men are not the only sexual beings. Acts of lovemaking are carnal, mental, emotional, and spiritual. Let God lead you into the promised land of intimacy. Yes, this glorious terrain includes heart-racing passion, but it offers so much more.

Genuine connection, when you're at peace in each other's presence.

The *knowing* and *feeling* of being one with your husband.

Authentic affection, outdoing one another with intimate expressions of honor.[15]

God brings water to your desert places. Allow yourself to be vulnerable before him, and ask him to show you a glimpse of the blessing, what it looks like for your marriage mountains to drip with sweet wine. Visualize the dry places in your relationship flowing with water from the house of the Lord.

Turn your heart to your husband and assume the exclusive role of his lover, the one his heart yearns for. Together, you share intimate passion, adding kindling to a private fire.

Wifestyle: Subdued or Spicy

The subdued wife finds herself unfulfilled. She struggles to enjoy times of connecting with her husband as their interactions always seem stifled, stressed, or one-sided. She hasn't found the courage to be fully exposed before her mate, and undisclosed issues and insecurities hinder their relationship.

The spicy wife embraces her sex life. She chooses intimacy over any lesser role and is marked by openness, confidence, and tenacious fun in their marital relationship. She talks comfortably with her husband about her intimate needs—physical and otherwise—and relishes in the freedom of their pleasurable encounters.

Is Your Wifestyle Subdued or Spicy?

Complete this wifestyle quiz to personalize the themes of this chapter in a practical way. Please circle the responses below that best represent your answer to each question.

	A	B
Lovemaking is a chore, not a pleasurable experience.	True	False
My husband is a sexual being. I'm not.	True	False
I promise sex to encourage certain actions in my husband.	True	False
I support my husband in ways he finds annoying.	True	False
I carry unrealistic "sexpectations" based on sinful experiences or Hollywood fantasies.	True	False
Please circle words in each column that best describe your recent attitudes or behaviors toward your husband. Circle all that apply.	Parental Stressed Closed off	Aroused Connected Exposed

Please tally your results. If you have more "A" answers, you're exhibiting a stronger subdued wifestyle. "B" answers show a stronger spicy wifestyle. Don't let this chapter or the issues we discussed discourage you. God wants to do a new thing in your marriage, and it can start today!

Ways to Spice Up Your Wife Life
Explore these ideas as you grow in intimacy with your husband:

- Talk with your man about sexual impurities, expectations, insecurities, injuries, and areas of enjoyment. Seek unity and health in sexual intimacy. Purity in your sex life doesn't mean boring intercourse. Sometimes it's intimidating to talk about sex, but you must communicate to find mutual satisfaction in this area of your marriage.

- When we view our husbands as children, the real issue is often in how we see ourselves. Ask God to change your perspective about yourself and to help you to regard yourself as a vibrant, sexy bride.

- Talk with your husband about how to best communicate as his helpmate. I removed many mothering tendencies by asking Jared in advance if he wants my help.

- Step back from all the activity and watch your husband with the perspective of a passionate lover. Who is this man you partnered for the rest of your life? What traits do you find attractive? Store the perspective of a lover in your heart and speak of it often.

- Do you struggle with extreme modesty? Ask God to speak with you about areas of insecurity or misunderstandings you've had about modesty's role in your marriage.

- Seek to outdo your husband with intimate consideration. Prefer him and seek to heighten his pleasure. If he's not good at reciprocating the kindness, share your desires in a time, place, and manner that edify your relationship.

What Do You Think?

- Have you focused on other areas of intimacy (emotional, spiritual, intellectual) and disregarded the value of physical intimacy in your marriage?

- Do you believe God wants to give you an incredible sex life?

- Have you let your mind and heart wander away from your husband? If so, what activities need to change as you turn back to him?
- Are there areas of your life that you withhold from your husband under the guise of propriety?
- Are there ways you assume the role of your husband's mother rather than his wife? (If you really want to know, ask your husband!)

Real Life #Wifestylin: Lisa N.'s Story

I came into marriage with wounds from past rejections and insecurities, so I found it difficult to bring up hard conversations or to say, "I'm sorry." Those events made me feel vulnerable, and in the past, being open lead to being hurt.

In our first two years of marriage, we lost two babies to miscarriage. Our intimacy staggered because I began to shut myself off to both physical and emotional love. My husband didn't respond to my grief like I thought he should, driving that wedge even deeper. We both put up walls and rarely communicated our feelings and need for intimacy. Our marriage was being sucked dry and I knew God was calling me to be vulnerable again, but I refused.

After two years of this crazy cycle, we began to see a counselor. We needed help making our marriage a safe place. Going to counseling opened my eyes to some hard truths about myself and the role I played in damaging our relationship. One of my deepest desires has always been to have a marriage that reflects Jesus to others, so it broke my heart that we were in this unhealthy place. God told me I needed to be vulnerable first or our marriage would quickly unravel. So I started speaking the word "restoration" over our intimacy and choosing actions aligned with obedience to his instruction. His strength is made perfect in my weakness, and I really started to believe this and rely on him.

Being vulnerable has transformed our marriage. My heart has changed in my thoughts about sex and trusting my husband. The connection we now share, emotionally and physically, is rooted deeper and will only become stronger. It's always a work in progress. My flesh resists, but my spirit wins because it is strengthened in the presence of my Savior.

–Lisa N., married in 2010

Lisa realized that her perspectives and actions hindered her relational intimacy. The marriage she had was not the marriage she wanted, or the best of what God had for her. Through counseling, she worked to overcome her fears and past wounds by applying God's truth to her life and believing him for restoration. While this transformation takes time, Lisa is already seeing the fruit of God's faithfulness in the deeper emotional and physical intimacy she shares with her husband.

CHAPTER ELEVEN

The *Blessing* of Life as a Godly Wife

"Most blessed among women . . ."

Judges 5:24

I come to this final chapter filled with hope.

Some desires are silly; wishing you won't picture me as a slob, with all my real life revelations about unwashed hair.

Most are grand aspirations.

I hope you heard God through these pages, and that you'll find the confidence to trust what he says to you.

The Lord offers hidden riches in secret places—through narrow gates where only few enter,[1] to make known the mysteries of his will and the hope of a better inheritance.[2] He invites us to seek and find, knocking on closed doors that he may open them.[3] The God of endurance and encouragement calls us to unity,[4] exhorting us to stockpile rewards in heaven—for where our treasure is, there we place our hearts also.[5]

These verses are about the whole of the gospel. The full truth of Jesus. Incomparable grace and peace, mercy, love, restoration, salvation, and forgiveness, found in the character of God and in communion with his spirit.

Our marriages are a small part of our walk of faith, but that doesn't mean we can discount the truth of the Bible because we dislike an area of application. Receiving the blessing of life as a godly wife requires that we follow God's instruction for our *lives* as *wives*. Some of us want to set the topics in this book aside as trivial, a message not meant for us. We want to believe we can love and serve and worship in full-hearted devotion to God without receiving these things for our marriages. However,

- If these humble pages and stories prick something in your spirit . . .
- When you recall a marriage moment where you could have chosen a better path . . .
- If you feel God prompting your heart to make a change . . .
- When the Lord says, "Daughter, listen here . . ."

> The Lord includes your marriage in the expression of your faith.

That, my friend, is conviction. Now, cheek-to-cheek with God's instruction, I hope you find the blessing of a godly wife in how you obey. Take your thoughts and actions captive in obedience to Christ.[6] The Lord includes your marriage in the expression of your faith.

Contemplate what we've talked about and search Scripture. Seek counsel as you find practical application. Don't fall into the trap of hearing the truth and not doing what it says—for when we persevere to act according to his Word, we are blessed in the doing.[7] Those who are steadfast in faith lack nothing.[8]

Could you use another form of confirmation? Verification that God wants you on this path toward his blessings? Evidence of his will?

> We ask you, [sisters], to respect those who labor among
> you and are over you in the Lord and admonish you,
> and to esteem them very highly in love because of their
> work. Be at peace among yourselves. And we urge you,
> [sisters], admonish the idle [or disorderly], encourage
> the fainthearted, help the weak, be patient with them all.
> See that no one repays anyone evil for evil, but always
> seek to do good to one another and to everyone. Rejoice
> always, pray without ceasing, give thanks in all circum-
> stances; for this is the will of God in Christ Jesus for you.
> (1 Thess. 5:12–18)

Receive

Sometimes I come to God as a reluctant child.

"OK. I guess. If I have to."

God's not forcing us to eat broccoli here. He's offering the things our hearts desire.

Intimacy.

Security.

Connection.

Provision.

No one suffers through a blessing; they're honored by it. The roles the Lord gives us in our marriages, and the parts our husbands play, these are positions to celebrate, not tolerate. String up the lights and cue the singing; we are living proof of who God is.

Receive the blessing of life as a godly wife. Jesus wants to show off in your marriage. Compensating for the areas you lack. Restoring desolate places. Answering the secret prayers of your heart, even the ones you haven't dared to speak out loud.

> Jesus wants to show off in your marriage.

He leads us in paths of righteousness for his name's sake, causing us to find rest in bug-free meadows, lounging beside quiet freshwater pools. His presence keeps us secure even at terrifying heights and in horrifying valleys. We eat lavish feasts in the face of our enemies. Revived in spirit, our cups brim over with abundance.[9]

Don't approach the favor of God with fearful trepidation. Run headlong into it! Contribute to your safe haven, crafting a marriage interwoven with Jesus—a partnership punctuated by your peace, prayer, and gratitude. Believe your husband can serve as a good leader in your home. Be determined to receive and honor him as an authority figure placed by God in the most intimate corners of your life. Choose the more excellent way. Let God be the source of all things good in your marriage.

Forget the empty work of trying to tape happy things to your outsides while you're hurt and wounded on the inside.

I don't want a clanging cymbal of a marriage.[10] I can work so hard to *be* patient and speak with kindness, to catch arrogant words before they escape and struggle not to insist on my own way, supergluing the symptoms of love to my life.

Or I can just *receive* him, the one they call Love.

Leave tedious short-lived success behind. We waste so much energy trying to figure out how to make things look good instead of just receiving *good* from the one who is. Breathe in his truth as oxygen to your spirit and let it exhale out of you as life to your relationships.

Our gender finds itself in the devastating aftermath of war. We hear horror stories of atrocities. Abuse. Mistreatment. Women treated as lesser-than, silent observers, and muted participants in their own lives.

So we grow up gun-shy. A car backfires in the distance, and we think *bomb*. We feel that's all we've known, when in truth, that's all we've trained our eyes to see. We find solace in the chance to be in charge, defining our lives and successes by societal standards, not heavenly ones. Risk averse, we avoid vulnerability, letting undisclosed issues and insecurities hinder our relationships. We struggle to trust while stressing over our lack of support and resources.

When we group the instruction and promises of God in with the lies of the enemy, we throw away the shield that protects us. We send out drone strikes on things like marital submission and husband-leadership, not realizing that *we* are the unfortunate targets.

Don't tiptoe up to the edge of God's blessings, hoping for a drop of rain, when you can dance in a waterfall. Invest your energy, thoughts, emotions, and expectations in what will happen when God proves faithful. He always follows through with the *doing*. We come with the *believing*.

> Don't tiptoe up to the edge of God's blessings, hoping for a drop of rain, when you can dance in a waterfall.

Position yourself to receive God's supply by how you obey his instruction. Often, receiving the next piece of instruction, fresh calling, or new inspiration first requires that we respond to the last direction he gave us.

And sometimes, accessing his blessings is as simple as stepping out in faith in the circumstance he puts before us.

Tent Pegs

In Judges chapter 4, the Israelites experience twenty years of oppression at the hands of King Jabin, his army commander, Sisera, and his nine hundred chariots of iron. The people cry to the Lord for help, and on the day of battle, God delivers the enemy militia into their hands. Only the commander escapes, fleeing on foot.

In Jen's version, I imagine Sisera running with nowhere to turn. His military might stripped away, he stumbles through creeks and dry ravines. Aimless and exhausted, this tyrant begins to despair. Then he remembers his king's associate. He recalls their visits to Heber's tent, and the pleasant accommodations they enjoyed. The gentle breeze as they made business deals under the shade of an oak tree, waited on hand and foot by Heber's hot wife.

Sisera finds his bearings and hurries toward the ally, the Israelite army in quick pursuit. No time to stop and look for water, the commander's dry throat aches by the time he sees the camp.

Now Heber's wife, Jael, saw Sisera coming. His haphazard running made him easy to spot in the distance, staggering from tree to tree like a man accustomed to travel by chariot. She fixes her hair before stepping out to greet him, welcoming him into her tent with soothing words. A hospitable host, she covers him with a cozy blanket and offers him warm milk.

Sisera's eyes close as he finds comfort in his new hiding place. "Stand watch," he tells her. "If a man comes by, he's my enemy; tell him I'm not here."

But no *male* adversary approaches.

Jael stands, watching *him*, not the opening to the tent, until her opponent is fast asleep. With gentle hands, she moves the empty bowl and folds back the blanket—no need to get blood on those things. There, the tenderness stops. In one swooping motion, Jael grabs a tent peg and mallet. Placing the spike over his temple, she swings the hammer high with her right hand and drives the stake straight through his skull. Into. The. Ground.[11]

. . . And the land had rest for forty years. (Judg. 5:31)

The enemy approached Jael, assuming things were status quo. That he'd have his run of the place, as he did before. He discounted her strength, resolve, and awareness of the situation.

But Jael, that woman put a literal stake in the ground. She aligned herself with the will of God and removed the oppressor from her camp.

Friends, we're standing here with tent pegs and the question must be asked: What are we going to do with them?

Heritage

Each generation, era, and tribe faces their own Siseras—adversaries who make themselves comfortable while the other family members lack rest. Once trusted allies, someone steps up to make a change. To expose the enemy and kick him out of the camp. Or drive home a tent peg.

Sometimes it takes awhile to recognize the opposition, since our enemy isn't flesh and blood.[12] Sisera is welcome in all the other tents on the block. We see his symbolic image in aged family photos, arms linked with generations of wives who each fought this submission, honor, respect thing in their own way.

Unless we've made an intentional choice toward a different path, much of our view of the world comes from our parents—both good and bad. We inherited the *right way* to fold towels, load the dishwasher, and make chicken soup. Their examples guided our formative years, and the same observation that taught us how to pronounce our vowels or swing our hips also informed our approach to marriage. We gained familial tendencies in how to communicate, what to hide, where and when to allow vulnerability, and what passes as acceptable actions in our relationships.

Melding two lives into one further complicates things, as your husband comes with different life lessons and experiences. Add a concoction of misguided gender roles, fears, and societal tendencies toward anarchy, and your loving home may need the insurance policy of a mad scientist's lair. This isn't an attack on our families; it's a chance to appreciate the good and toss out the bad of what we've seen before.

Most women don't recognize the harm in fighting for leadership roles. We think it's only natural to fend for ourselves and deflect covering out of preference for independence. Generations of well-intentioned women steal their mates' manhood by undermining his role in their lives. Like a bad family photo, everything looks off and a bit creepy. For once it's not the awkward Christmas sweaters. Sisera is in the camp.

That's the *before* picture.

I think of all these tendencies that I have: Attempting to craft my husband into my image. Walking in fear and timidity instead of faith-filled confidence. Running here and there, frayed, unraveled, exhausted in trying to put on an identity instead of receiving one. Cleaving to my past instead of to my husband. Coaching, not confiding. Living as a spousal parent, not a lover. Advocating for my dreams and fighting for authority instead of walking in agreement under it. When I stop to consider all these things, I'm faced with a greater reality. How I live today holds eternal implications.

What do I want the *after* snapshot to look like?

What if my children, their children, and their children's children inherited a different behavior? A lineage of women who reject the accepted narrative of *strength* as *control*. Women confident in their femininity. Who accept covering as a good thing. Not afraid to walk under authority because they recognize the benefits of genuine leadership.

I envision boys growing into men as they watch their mothers honor their fathers and fathers sacrifice with limitless abandon, setting new expectations for healthy marriages and giving our sons higher standards for their future wives.

I'm modeling a lifestyle, a wifestyle, for my children. My actions teach them how to view God and how to honor authority. I want my example to emulate hope and love so they notice the blessings of the Lord's faithfulness in my life. To gaze upon Jesus—living, breathing, walking, and talking on earth—and not just in my parenting or external ministry, but in my marriage.

BONUS: Download the printable "Prayer for My Children's Future Spouses" at thejenweaver.com/wifestylebonus

Celebrating

I love the story of Jael because she doesn't wait for her man to step in and do something. Too often as wives, we hold on to conflicting storylines:

I'm a brave, strong woman, no man is going to keep me down. I make my own choices, choose my own path.

Oh . . .

Submission? Trust God with my marriage? Choose grace and unity?

I'll do that if my husband goes first. We need to work on our marriage together. If he does his part, I'll do mine.

> Friend, you are a strong, brave woman. Pick up your tent peg.

I hope your husband does those things for you. I want him to go before, leading the charge with his own heart change and servant leadership. But friend, you are a strong, brave woman. Pick up your tent peg.

We don't have to sit around waiting for something else to happen before we access the blessings of our loving Father. We are princesses, a royal priesthood, carriers of his presence.

Jael took care of Sisera all by herself. Her man came home that day and noticed something different about his tent. Or maybe it took awhile for him to realize the change. Months later, he comments to Jael over appetizers at the local watering hole: "Something is different about you. About us. About this place. There's a sense of rest and peace. Things are good, better than I've felt before . . . Hey, whatever happened to Jabin's commander? I noticed he's not around anymore."

She smiles. "Oh, I took care of him."

Jael approached the situation with full-hearted effort, removing all chance for Sisera to ever return. She lived as a recipient of the blessing.

> "Most blessed among women is Jael, The wife of Heber
> the Kenite . . ." (Judg. 5:24 NKJV)

In a world of *not enough*, and marriages settling for *good enough*, press further into God and receive his *more-than-enough*.[13] Your marriage presents the opportunity to align your life with the authority of heaven, requiring choices, character, and commitments of brave faith. Recognize that your spousal relationship is created for something more than what you've ever known or experienced.

> In a world of *not enough*, and marriages settling for *good enough*, press further into God and receive his *more-than-enough*.

Choose to celebrate the honor of being a wife. You are mighty in valor. Patient. Gracious. Forgiving. You fend off perspectives that come against the blessings of God, and you fight for your marriage without ceasing—refusing to settle for less than what Jesus has for you. You agree with his truth and proclaim it over your life through prayer and obedience.

Trustworthy and full of faith, you believe the Lord's promises. You, my friend, are steadfast. Confident. Assured of who God is, you receive divine provision from his hand. Hope, encouragement, and love cover your family like a blanket. The blessing of life as a godly wife brings you strength in difficulty. You have peace during trials because everywhere you go, you carry the presence of Jesus. You live victorious.

Fellow warriors, my hope is that these words resonate in your spirit. Proclaim them; true descriptions of the life, the wifestyle, and the blessings God holds out before you. Stake down your disappointments, hurts, and fears. They hold no influence in your life any longer. The next time you see a negative habit, perspective, or tendency creeping in to undermine the Lord's favor in your life, look the enemy dead in the eyes and grab a tent peg.

BONUS: Download the "Tent Peg Worksheet"
at thejenweaver.com/wifestylebonus

Wifestyle: Pessimist or Party

A pessimist wife is skeptical that God's Word will prove true in her life and lacks confidence that his model for marriage can work for her relationship. She remains stuck on what her husband needs to change and finds it unfair that she would need to do her part to submit while he's still struggling in other areas.

The party wife walks in full assurance. She celebrates opportunities to grow into the wife the Lord designed her to be. Through her actions and renewed perspective, this wife sees transformation in her husband and in her spousal relationship. She establishes a new heritage for her children, redefining what it means to be a wife, and choosing a new path for her family's future because of the way she obeys God's instruction for her marriage.

Is Your Wifestyle Pessimist or Party?

Personalize the themes of this chapter by circling the responses below that best represent your answer to each question.

	A	B
It's not worth working on my marriage unless my husband is going to make changes too.	True	False
I don't think disregarding God's instruction for my marriage will impact my relationship with him.	True	False
Submission is fine for other people, but it doesn't work for me.	True	False
Husband-leadership isn't practical.	True	False
I tolerate God's instruction in this area of my life, but there's no way I can celebrate it.	True	False
Please circle words in each column that best describe your recent attitudes or behaviors toward your husband. Circle all that apply.	Uncertain Disheartened Dismissive	Faith-filled Courageous Expectant

Please tally your results. "A" answers fall on the pessimist wifestyle spectrum. "B" answers show a party wifestyle. Even if you've gone through this entire book and find only areas of improvement through these wifestyle quizzes, God never condemns. He forgives freely and invites you to begin today with a fresh start. Use the themes in these chapters, the quizzes, application steps, and questions to help you draw closer to God and your husband—not push you further away.

Ways to Plan a Party

Here are some ways to grow in your life as a faith-filled party wife:

- Give thanks in advance for the things you know God will do in your life, for your husband, and for your marriage.
- List the changes you are grateful for in your own heart. Add to the list as you watch the Lord move in your spouse.
- Write out some character qualities you want your children to see in you. What do you want them to look for in their future mates? Pray these attributes into being.
- Consider what Siseras may be in your family camp. Ask the Lord to show you how your actions can kick them out.

What Do You Think?

- What areas would you want to improve in your marriage if your children used you as an example for the type of spouse they wanted to become—or the type of wife they'd like to find?
- What actions or attitudes have become "normal" in your relationship but are really signs of the enemy's presence in your marriage camp?
- Has God brought personal conviction through specific topics we've discussed? If so, have you responded in obedience, or are you dragging your feet?
- Do you live as though being a submitted wife is a noble calling?

Real Life #Wifestylin: Karen's Story

The enemy is out to steal, kill, and destroy families. After twenty-six years of marriage and six kids, my husband left. John's heart had been hardening for years as he lost interest in me and in our family. I tried everything to stop him, yet he slipped away, entangled in secret sin, addiction, and betrayal.

In those troubled years, conflict permeated our marriage. I thought if I did certain things or looked a certain way, I could change him. I couldn't. I'd bounce between emotional outbursts and demure appease-ment without understanding what submission meant or how to communicate in healthy ways. I became apprehensive to speak up at all, so I resigned to tol-erating everything, out of fear of losing my marriage.

John left and I broke. After years of trying to do things the way I thought God wanted, or the way others had done them, I was ready for the work he wanted to do in me. I gave my whole heart to the Lord, and entrusted him with my husband's as well. I went to counseling and found my worth again in Christ. God did some really deep work in my heart, teaching me about identity, trust, and healthy, loving boundaries.

I'd told our kids about Jesus their entire lives and knew they were watching my actions. Now it was time for me to tangibly live out my faith before them. Even though my husband broke our vows, I felt God's call for me to remain steadfast and pray for my marriage. He spoke softly to my heart, "Wait on me, not your husband." So I stood in the gap for my family while I waited on his timing, trusting God with whatever outcome he thought best.

I learned later that during our eighteen-month separation, my husband battled conflict within himself. The things he thought would make him happy did little to satisfy him. He recommitted his life to Christ, and God turned John's heart back to me. My husband realized I loved him in a way he'd never experienced before by another human—a beautiful and painful realization. He came to my house one October night, and we began the process of healing. In deep crisis, we struggled to see a future of redemption. But day by day, we walked by faith. Together. As we did, the Lord redeemed everything.

Now, with over thirty-four years of marriage, including the restored broken years, John and I stand as witnesses to God's faithfulness. Recipients of his unending grace in the midst of our darkest days, I'm grateful for God's transformation in our hearts. The Lord taught me to stand firm on his truth even when it felt like the enemy had won. Battle is never easy, but marriage is worth fighting for—especially when that fighting looks like obedience to Jesus's gentle whispers and patiently waiting before God in prayer. Victory is always the Lord's.

–Karen Rellos, married in 1982 (redeeming-love.com)

Your Story

God wants to bring his truth to real life application in your life. Talk with him about practical ways he wants you to apply wifestyle habits in your interactions with your husband. Take note of the fruit produced by your obedience. The return may seem small or slow coming at first, but don't give up. God *always* proves faithful.

As you watch and see an increase of the Lord's blessings in your life and marriage, I'd love to hear your testimony! Please share your story with our team at thejenweaver.com/wifestylin.

Additional Resources

Visit thejenweaver.com/wifestylebonus for free BONUS resources on the topics we discussed in *A Wife's Secret to Happiness*.

Notes

Chapter One

[1] Psalm 84:7
[2] 2 Corinthians 3:16–18
[3] Ephesians 3:19–20
[4] Jeremiah 29:11–14 NIV
[5] Ecclesiastes 4:9–12 NIV
[6] Mark 10:9 NIV
[7] Philippians 2:3–4 NIV
[8] Ephesians 4:32 NIV
[9] Ecclesiastes 4:9–12
[10] Jeremiah 23:23–24
[11] Matthew 7:7–11, James 1:17
[12] Philippians 4:7
[13] 1 Corinthians 13:7
[14] James 4:2–3
[15] 2 Kings 5:1–14

Chapter Two

[1] Genesis 2:18
[2] Matthew 18:20
[3] Ecclesiastes 4:9
[4] Henry, Matthew. *An Exposition of the Old and New Testament* (Philadelphia: Haswell, Barrington & Haswell, 1838).
[5] Ecclesiastes 4:10
[6] Ephesians 5:25
[7] Genesis 2:24

[8] Ephesians 5:26
[9] Ephesians 5:27
[10] James 5:16
[11] Ephesians 5:27
[12] Ephesians 6:1
[13] John 10:10

Chapter Three

[1] Ephesians 5:22–24, 1 Peter 3:1, 1 Corinthians 11:3, and Colossians 3:18.
[2] Matthew 8
[3] Daniel 7:13–14, Matthew 28:18
[4] Luke 10:10
[5] Ephesians 5:22
[6] Hebrews 13:17
[7] Psalm 84:10 NIV
[8] Genesis 3:1 NIV
[9] Luke 22:42
[10] Morris, Debbie. *The Blessed Woman: A Timeless Journey with Women of the Bible* (Southlake, TX: Gateway Create Publishing, 2012), 100.
[11] Sanders, J. Oswald. *Spiritual Leadership: Principles of Excellence for Every Believer,* 2nd revision (Chicago: The Moody Bible Institute, 1994), 131–132.
[12] Exodus 3:7–8

[13] Exodus 10:11 NIV
[14] Ephesians 5:24
[15] Exodus 14:10–12 NIV
[16] Jeremiah 29:11–14 NIV
[17] 1 Samuel 2:30
[18] 1 Samuel 26:23

Chapter Four
[1] Hebrews 11:6
[2] Mark 12:14
[3] 1 Samuel 16
[4] Exodus 4:10
[5] Matthew 4:18–22
[6] Matthew 9:9
[7] Genesis 12:10–20, Genesis 20.
[8] Genesis 12:2
[9] Genesis 15:5
[10] Genesis 17
[11] Hebrews 11:11
[12] Mark 5:27

Chapter Five
[1] Proverbs 14:1
[2] James 4:6
[3] Ephesians 5:25
[4] 2 Corinthians 6:14
[5] 1 Peter 4:8
[6] 1 Corinthians 3:7–9
[7] James 1:5
[8] Matthew 6:32
[9] Psalm 84:11
[10] Ephesians 3:20

Chapter Six
[1] From James Strong, *Strong's Expanded Exhaustive Concordance of the Bible* (Nashville: Thomas Nelson, 2009). Strong's Lexicon

H242: "לְיִח, chayil, khah'-yil; from H2342; probably a force, whether of men, means or other resources; an army, wealth, virtue, valor, strength:— able, activity, ( ) army, band of men (soldiers), company, (great) forces, goods, host, might, power, riches, strength, strong, substance, train, ( ) valiant(-ly), valour, virtuous(-ly), war, worthy(-ily)."
[2] Proverbs 31:21
[3] Proverbs 31:10–31
[4] Psalm 103:4
[5] Isaiah 62
[6] 2 Timothy 2:20–21
[7] Book of Esther
[8] Proverbs 31:10 NIV
[9] Titus 2:4–5 NIV
[10] Proverbs 31
[11] Titus 2:5 NIV
[12] Amos 3:3 NIV

Chapter Seven
[1] 1 Peter 3:1–2
[2] 1 Timothy 5:17
[3] Ephesians 5:33
[4] 1 Peter 3:7
[5] Luke 6:45
[6] 1 Peter 3:15, 2 Chronicles 16:9
[7] James 3:12
[8] James 3:8
[9] James 3:5
[10] Proverbs 14:1
[11] Proverbs 18:21
[12] Ephesians 4:29
[13] Ephesians 4:23
[14] Eldredge, John. *Wild at Heart: Discovering the Secret of a Man's Soul* (Nashville: Yates & Yates LLP, 2001), 48.

[15] Isaiah 64:8

[16] Genesis 2:7

[17] Genesis 1:27

[18] Psalm 127:1

[19] Psalm 118:8

[20] 1 Corinthians 2:4

[21] Jeremiah 17:9

[22] James 3:6

[23] Proverbs 14:12

[24] 1 Corinthians 8:1

[25] 1 John 4:8

[26] Genesis 35:10

[27] Matthew 16:18

[28] Genesis 17:5

[29] Genesis 17:15

[30] Genesis 1:1–2 *The Message*

[31] Judges 6:12

[32] 1 Samuel 16:7

[33] 1 Samuel 16

[34] 1 Corinthians 1:17

[35] 1 Corinthians 14:3

[36] 1 Corinthians 14:3

Chapter Eight

[1] Matthew 12:25

[2] Philippians 2:2–4

[3] Jeremiah 29:11

[4] Jeremiah 29:12–13

[5] Luke 2:19

[6] Joshua 6:20

[7] Joshua 5:13–14 *The Message*

[8] Joshua 1:7–8

[9] Luke 11:2

[10] Job 38:35

[11] Job 38:10

[12] Matthew 6:33–34

[13] Hebrews 13:17

[14] James 1:17

[15] Ephesians 3:20 NKJV

[16] Matthew 6:33

[17] Luke 11:28

[18] Hebrews 10:23

[19] Romans 8:28

[20] 1 Samuel 17:33, 1 Samuel 16:12

[21] 1 Samuel 18

[22] Genesis 37–41

[23] Psalm 37

[24] Jeremiah 29:13–14

Chapter Nine

[1] 1 Peter 2:9

[2] Hebrews 4:14–5:10

[3] 1 Peter 2:9

[4] Hebrews 7:25

[5] Ephesians 2:20–22

[6] Matthew 18:24

[7] Psalm 130:3–4

[8] Matthew 6:9–15

[9] Luke 6:38

[10] Genesis 4:1

[11] Matthew 5:37

[12] Ephesians 6:4, Proverbs 22:6

[13] Ecclesiastes 4:9–10

[14] Ephesians 4:29

[15] 1 Corinthians 12

[16] Colossians 3:13 NLT

Chapter Ten

[1] Song of Solomon 1:9, 4:1, 7:4, 7:2

[2] Joel 2:13 *The Message*

[3] Exodus 20:17

[4] Colossians 3:18, Ephesians 5:22

[5] 1 Timothy 2:9 NIV

6 Slattery, Juli. *25 Questions You're Afraid to Ask About Love, Sex, and Intimacy* (Chicago, Moody Publishers, 2015), 78–84.

7 1 Corinthians 7:2, 1 Corinthians 6:16

8 Galatians 5:19, Romans 13:13

9 Leviticus 18:22, Leviticus 20:13, Romans 1:27, 1 Corinthians 6:9

10 Ephesians 5:25–29

11 1 Peter 3:7. The Greek word for "dwell with" is συνοικέω and means (a) to live with domestically and (b) marital intercourse. One possible interpretation of that passage is that husbands are to honor their wives in the way they experience lovemaking.

12 1 Corinthians 7:5

13 Hebrews 13:4

14 1 Corinthians 7:5

15 Romans 12:10

Chapter Eleven

1 Matthew 7:13

2 Ephesians 1:9–11

3 Matthew 7:7

4 Romans 15:5–7

5 Matthew 6:19–21

6 2 Corinthians 10:5

7 James 1:22–25

8 James 1:4

9 Psalm 23

10 1 Corinthians 13:1

11 Judges 4

12 Ephesians 6:12

13 Psalm 4:7 *The Message*

Acknowledgments

Jesus, thank you for entrusting me with this message. At times, I've wished you came with a more popular concept, or at least something easier for me to learn. More than once, I tried to prove you wrong before trusting your words enough to apply them to my own marriage. As these truths produced fruit in my life, I then questioned your strategy in giving such vital insight to a newbie author with a tiny platform. Even still, you didn't take it away, but waited patiently for me. For that I am humbled and forever grateful.

Jared, you I love. I respect you more than anyone I've ever known. Thank you for setting the goal in your heart to love me like Christ loves the church, and for choosing me as your wife. You've always believed in me, believed in us, and supported God's call on my life. I'm honored to call you my leader, my love, my best friend, and my first beta reader. For the rest of our lives, baby!

Dillon, you are my sunshine. The gift of your existence contributed to this book in ways you'll never fully know. I love you, and I pray your future wife will live these words even better than I.

Most heartfelt gratitude for . . .

My parents, for always believing God had great things for me and encouraging me to know him.

My family—and the friends I love like family—for your unwavering encouragement and for jumping in as my sounding boards at a moment's notice. Thank you for letting me be me. So often, our times together are just what I need, and God knows this. Special thanks and a sister hug to Stephanie. I love how close we've grown and how you keep social media from taking over my life.

My support team, for your help with all the back-end online techie things, and for reading all my lengthy emails. Your diligent effort frees my focus.

My fellow writers and bloggers, and my critique group lead by the invaluable Lena Nelson Dooley, for reviewing the *many* first drafts of this manuscript with encouragement and diligent red pens. And my writing mentors, Julie Marx and Bonnie Wilks— you've helped me wrap this book in love and always turn my focus to Jesus. You've all called more out of me than I even knew was in there and helped me find my voice.

My online readers, we are real life friends in my head. I think of you and pray blessings for you often. I'm honored that you've joined me on this writing journey, and your testimonies of life change fill my heart. I love sharing strength with you.

My incredible family at Gateway Church—led in Word and example by Pastor Robert Morris—especially Pastors Jan Greenwood, Lynda Grove, Stephanie and Allan Kelsey, Aaron Wronko, and Brad Stahl, for your ministry and friendship. I'm in full ugly cry right now as I consider the ways you've encouraged, empowered, and equipped me to walk in obedience to my Father. Jan, this book title is a gift from your guidance. Thank you. Laurinda Dunn, for being the first person to read my manuscript from beginning to end, for your helpful feedback, and for holding it with such grace.

Exceptional thanks also to . . .

A Wife's Secret to Happiness testimony writers, for sharing your powerful words. Each and every story touched my heart and bolstered my faith for what God wants to do in our marriages.

The book endorsers, for carving out the time to help me get this book into the hands of readers. I'm grateful for your support.

The countless authors and speakers, pastors, and teachers, who've helped shape my perspective of God, marriage, and submission. Your diligent study and poignant words inspire me to seek the Lord and continually develop my craft.

Blythe Daniel, for being my champion and my agent. You're a blessing to have in my corner.

The team at Leafwood Publishers, for taking a risk and investing in this message. I'm grateful for your partnership.

Gateway WILD women, my Declare Team, and the Declare Community—you are beautiful. Your wild obedience inspires me daily.

And, finally, to all who pray out these words, who stand beside me proclaiming the truths of this book over our lives and marriages—thank you.